How to use

C000160702

In this issue

The 90 daily readings in this issue of *Explore* are designed to help you understand and apply the Bible as you read it each day.

It's serious!

We suggest that you allow 15 minutes each day to work through the Bible passage with the notes. It should be a meal, not a snack! Readings from other parts of the Bible can throw valuable light on the study passage. These cross-references can be skipped if you are already feeling full up, but they will expand your grasp of the Bible. *Explore* uses the NIV2011 Bible translation, but you can also use it with the NIV1984 or ESV translations.

Sometimes a prayer box will encourage you to stop and pray through the lessons—but it is always important to allow time to pray for God's Spirit to bring his word to life, and to shape the way we think and live through it.

We're serious!

All of us who work on Explore share a passion for getting the Bible into people's lives. We fiercely hold to the Bible as God's word— to honour and follow, not to explain away.

1 Find a time you can read the Bible each day

2 Find a place where you can be quiet and think

3 Ask God to help you understand

4 Carefully read through the Bible passage for today

5 Study the verses with Explore, taking time to think

6 Pray about what you have read

thegoodbook COMPANY

Opening up the Bible

Welcome to Explore

Being a Christian isn't a skill you learn, like carpentry or flower arranging. Nor is it a lifestyle choice, like the kind of clothes you wear, or the people you choose to hang out with. It's about having a real relationship with the living God through his Son, Jesus Christ. The Bible tells us that this relationship is like a marriage.

It's important to start with this, because many Christians view the practice of daily Bible-reading as a Christian duty, or a hard discipline that is just one more thing to get done in our busy modern lives.

But the Bible is God speaking to us: opening his mind to us on how he thinks, what he wants for us and what his plans are for the world. And most importantly, it tells us what he has done for us in sending his Son, Jesus Christ, into the world. It's the way the Spirit shows Jesus to us, and changes us as we behold his glory.

The Bible is not a manual. It's a love letter. And as with any love letter, we'll want to treasure it, and make time to read and re-read it, so we know we are loved, and discover how we can please the One who loves us. Here are a few suggestions for making your daily time with God more of a joy than a burden:

- *Time:* Find a time when you will not be disturbed, and when the cobwebs are cleared from your mind. Many people have found that the morning is the best time as it sets you up for the day. If you're not a "morning person", then last thing at night or a mid-morning break might suit you. Whatever works for you is right for you.

- *Place:* Jesus says that we are not to make a great show of our religion *(see Matthew 6:5-6)*, but rather, to pray with the door to our room shut. Some people plan to get to work a few minutes earlier and get their Bible out in an office or some other quiet corner.

- *Prayer:* Although *Explore* helps with specific prayer ideas from the passage, try to develop your own lists to pray through. Use the flap inside the back cover to help with this. And allow what you read in the Scriptures to shape what you pray for yourself, the world and others.

- *Share:* As the saying goes: *expression deepens impression.* So try to cultivate the habit of sharing with others what you have learned. Why not join our Facebook group to share your encouragements, questions and prayer requests? Search for *Explore: For your daily walk with God.*

And remember, *it's quality, not quantity, that counts:* better to think briefly about a single verse than to skim through pages without absorbing anything, because it's about developing your relationship with the living God. The sign that your daily time with God is real is when you start to love him more and serve him more wholeheartedly.

Tim Thornborough and Carl Laferton
Editors

REVELATION: Be faithful

Many people are confused by the cycles of "sevens" in John's book: seals, trumpets, thunders. Are they a sequence of events that will take place in history or something else?

These overlapping visions are not intended to be read sequentially but as different camera angles on the same events—the time in which John's readers lived and in which we live, leading up to the end of time. As we read these different sequences and images, John is saying, *it's a bit like this; or a bit like that; or it's something like this...* These visions should engage our imaginations and lead us to confidence in God's sovereignty rather than confusion and doubt.

Read Revelation 10:1-7

This new vision of the thunders interrupts the time between the sixth (9:13) and seventh trumpets; just as there was a gap between the sixth and seventh seals.

❷ *What does the description of the angel in verses 1-2 call to mind from the Bible?*

❷ *What happens when John hears the seven thunders (v 4)?*

❷ *What do you think the message they spoke may have been? (Hint: Think about the seals and the trumpets in chapters 6 – 9.)*

❷ *What are the two promises that are made in 10:6 and 7?*

❷ *What is "the mystery of God", do you think (v 7)?*

John is poised to catalogue the calamities that the thunders will bring—just as he's done with the seals and trumpets. But the seven thunders are immediately rescinded. It's not clear why, but it may be because humanity didn't respond to the seals and trumpets with repentance (9:20-21). The seven seals affected a quarter of the earth (6:8) while the seven trumpets affected a third of the earth (8:8-12; 9:15). Presumably the seven thunders would have affected a half of the earth. But the escalation of calamities in history will not bring repentance. So the thunders are withdrawn. Instead God reveals his secret weapon... represented by the tiny scroll in the angel's hand. It's seemingly so insignificant, and yet at the heart of God's purposes for the world.

Elsewhere in the New Testament, the mystery is a mystery no more for it's been revealed in the gospel of Christ (see Ephesians 3:8-11; Colossians 1:27). And the word "announced" in Revelation 10:7 is literally "evangelised". So the purposes of God in history revealed in the scroll involve the proclamation of the gospel by God's people. "There will be no more delay" (v 6) means there's no saving event that needs to happen before the final judgment (we've already had the cross, resurrection, ascension and Pentecost). There's nothing to stop Christ returning today. But "in the days when the seventh angel is about to sound his trumpet" (v 7)—that is, before the final judgment— the gospel is proclaimed to the nations.

⌃ Pray

Ask God to fulfil his purpose of gospel proclamation today, through your church, through missionaries... and through you.

Eating the scroll

John's description of what happens to the scroll would have been familiar to his readers from the Old Testament…

The scroll

Read Ezekiel 2:9 – 3:9 and then Revelation 10:8-11

- ❓ *What is the effect of the scroll on both Ezekiel and John?*
- ❓ *In verse 11 what is John told he must do as a result?*
- ❓ *How do you think this experience relates to our experience of receiving and sharing the gospel message?*
- ❓ *What would John's first readers have understood from the example and life of Ezekiel about the calling to be witnesses?*

Ezekiel proclaimed God's message faithfully to the exiles in Babylon—and images from his book and life are returned to again and again in Revelation. The message of the scroll is bittersweet for it is a message of victory through suffering. All Christians know something of John's experience. The message of Christ is so sweet to us. But this sweetness is matched by pain when family and friends reject the message, leaving a bitter taste in the stomach.

Revelation 10:11 is the key command in these chapters. And it extends beyond John to us. We must proclaim the gospel to the nations, even in the face of hostility. John is reminding us again and again that Christ's salvation and our mission extend across the globe. Just when we might be tempted to retreat in the face of hostility, John is repeatedly expanding our horizons. His message

to Christians is not that we should endure if by that we mean avoiding trouble by keeping our heads down. His message is to proclaim the gospel to nations, to peoples, to kings. Instead of his normal quartet of "nations, tribes, peoples and languages", John substitutes "kings" for "tribes". Yes, we even proclaim the gospel to kings—the holders of power and the source of threat.

☑ Apply

We are to withhold the gospel from no-one.

- ❓ *Who would you be fearful of sharing the gospel with? A Muslim perhaps? Or your boss at work?*

Our job now

Chapters 10 – 11 take place in a pause between the sixth and seventh trumpets. The seventh event in each of John's sequences describes the return of Christ and the final judgment. God has hit the pause button on his judgment. 2 Peter 3:9 says, "The Lord is not slow in keeping his promise, as some understand slowness. Instead, he is patient with you, not wanting anyone to perish, but everyone to come to repentance." The pause between the sixth and seventh trumpet—for as long as it lasts, and it will not last for ever—creates space for the mission of the church.

The measuring rod

Now John is given a measuring rod and is introduced to two witnesses who meet a grim end…

Measure the temple

Read Revelation 11:1-3

❓ *What do you think measuring the temple means?*

❓ *Why is the outer court left out?*

❓ *Who are the two witnesses, and what do the details in verse 3 represent?*

The temple that John is to measure is not a literal temple; it is a description of the church as it is now on earth. The measuring of the temple is a sign that, whatever happens in history, ultimately, the church is the safe place to be.

In the original temple the outer court was for the Gentiles: a promise of their inclusion. But now, in Christ, Jew and Gentile together are the temple (see Ephesians 2:11-22). So we don't need the outer court to symbolise inclusion, for that inclusion is a reality. Instead the outer court symbolises the threat posed by the unbelieving nations as they trample on God's people.

But the suffering of God's people will not last for ever. Forty-two months is a reference back to Daniel 7:25 ("a time, times and half a time" = a year, two years and half a year = "42 months" = "1,260 days"). John is reiterating the message of Daniel 7: whatever people may do to us, we are kept safe in history for eternity. But we are not passive in the face of hostility…

The witnesses

Read Revelation 11:4-10

❓ *What power have the two witnesses (also referred to as olive trees and lampstands) been given by God?*

❓ *What is brought to mind by the images in verse 6?*

❓ *What happens to them eventually?*

❓ *What is the reaction of the people to their deaths (v 9-10)?*

The two witnesses of verse 3 are God's people: his royal priesthood. Mission is both a priestly activity (representing God to the world) and a royal activity (extending Christ's reign by calling on people to submit to his authority). And through our words, we bring the fire of divine judgment on those who reject our message (see 2 Corinthians 2:15-16). To our priestly and kingly roles, we can add a prophetic role, since the two witnesses are also an allusion to the two greatest figures of the Old Testament: Moses and Elijah. Today, we are engaged in powerful word-ministry. For we bring either eternal life or eternal death as we proclaim the gospel. But we should not expect people to like us for it.

🔼 Pray

Pray that all who proclaim the good news of Jesus would understand the privilege and the cost of their calling—you too.

Resurrection power

We left the two witnesses yesterday dead and despised: rotting in the street, as people mock them and behaved as if it was Christmas. Now the tide turns…

The breath of life
Read Revelation 11:11-12

❓ *What happens next?*
❓ *What is the reaction of the bystanders?*
❓ *Where do the witnesses end up?*

The witnesses represent any and all individual Christians: churches (lampstands), or Christian leaders. We are protected from harm (v 5), so that we may proclaim the gospel, which is hated by those who hear it and opposed by the devil (the beast, v 7). The great city here is clearly Jerusalem, "where their Lord was crucified" (v 8). But ultimately it represents all cities anywhere where there are faithful Christians witnessing to the gospel of Christ and being opposed by Satan. In other words, *your* town.

The resurrection of the witnesses in verses 11-12 should not be understood as literal. It presents the truth of history as a whole: the church is persecuted, Christians are martyred, and at times the cause of Christ seems defeated. But the church survives and comes back with renewed strength, and the cause of Christ continues. What is God's "secret weapon" in the face of the hostile powers of this world? It is the faithful people of God sustained by the powerful Spirit of God. Again and again throughout history, regimes have risen and it's looked as if they would wipe out the church. But those regimes have gone and the church has come through persecution stronger. It

has been victorious through suffering. Life has come through death.

Fear and glory
Read Revelation 11:13

❓ *What happens to the city, and what is the ultimate response?*

The calamities of the seven seals and seven trumpets do not bring repentance (Revelation 9:20-21). Instead, the nations fear God and give him glory in response to the faithful witness of God's people—especially their faithful witness "even to the point of death" (2:10). Or perhaps sometimes it's the suffering witness of God's people combined with the calamities of history that brings people to repentance. The turmoil of history, represented by the seven seals and trumpets, on its own leads only to judgment. But the turmoil of history combined with Christian witness leads some to repentance.

🔼 Pray

Victory comes through suffering. Ask the Lord to imprint this truth in the minds of his people, so we will be prepared.

Turmoil can lead to repentance. Pray that those who are afflicted by suffering would also hear the gospel and see the faithfulness of Christian witnesses—and come to give glory to the God of heaven.

Victory song

After the interlude, at last, the seventh trumpet is blown, and the sounds of fear and hatred are replaced by a song of victory.

Everlasting victory

Read Revelation 11:14-19

❓ *What happens when the trumpet sounds?*

❓ *What is the tone or mood of what follows?*

❓ *What do the images of verse 19 bring to mind?*

❓ *Read over the victory song: what parts of it particularly appeal to you? Why?*

When the seventh trumpet sounds, the sequence of seven comes to an end and with it the course of history. In the end God is victorious. He will reign for ever (v 16-17). John draws attention to the ark in the temple (v 19). The ark contained the tablets of the covenant. So here John reminds us of God's faithfulness to his covenant promises: the nations will be judged and God's people will be rewarded (v 18). Despite all the calamities that befall the church in history, we are on the winning side.

But it's not a victory won through power or through the sword. It's not won through drone strikes nor by acts of terrorism. It's won by God's people witnessing to the gospel, even if that means weakness and death. Our model is Jesus, who in 1:5 is called "the faithful witness". He is the archetypal faithful witness even when it means death. This empire—"the kingdom of our Lord and of his Messiah" (11:15)—is won by the Lamb who was slain (5:6).

John's readers must have wondered if Christ was truly sovereign. They knew the stories of Nero's cruel persecutions in AD 64. They had witnessed the Parthian invasion, civil war in AD 69 ("the year of the four emperors"), the destruction of Jerusalem in AD 70, the eruption of Mount Vesuvius in AD 79 and the famines of AD 92. They knew the daily tension of a thousand choices to speak or keep quiet, to take a stand or participate in paganism. Revelation 6 – 11 shows that Christ rules over these sufferings. More than that, our sufferings are part of his plan to bring history under his rule.

Life through death

In these chapters God's people die and live. Because we're united to Christ, our lives are shaped by his death and resurrection. His death and resurrection are not just the means of our salvation; they're also the pattern for our lives. We die to self and live to God. Whenever you see people receiving spiritual life or a lively, living church, you can be sure that behind the scenes, often unnoticed, someone is working hard, denying themselves, making sacrifices.

⌄ Apply

❓ *Have you seen victory through suffering in your own experience?*

❓ *In what ways are you dying to yourself to bring life to others?*

Anxiety attack

This great song needs no introduction, except to say it's wonderful! As you read it try to work out why it has inspired and helped so many Christians down the years

Read Psalm 139

> ❓ *What moves you particularly about this psalm? What verse would you memorise from it and pass on to others today?*

Verses 19-22 are the clue to what's going on here. David is under attack from people who hate God and hate him. Scared and vulnerable, he stops to remember just how secure he is in God's hands.

God knows me

Re-read Psalm 139:1-6

> ❓ *How well does God know David (and therefore each of us)?*
> ❓ *What specifically does David recognise that God knows (v 4-6)?*

Such knowledge (v 5) might be terrifying to us, leading to paranoia, but verse 6 shows that David doesn't feel trapped by his lack of privacy from God.

God is everywhere

Re-read Psalm 139:7-10

David isn't trying to *escape* from God. Rather, he's just saying, *It's impossible to escape from God—even if I wanted to.*

···· TIME OUT ···

But there *are* times when we might want to run away from God... Sometimes, it's because we're harbouring some secret

sin that we don't want to have exposed to the Lord's disapproving (but loving) stare. Sometimes, we're just afraid of intimacy. But at other times, church, life, relationships, family even, all just get too much for us. We feel the pressures and demands, and react against being squeezed into a life that we didn't choose by work, family, friends and church. We lose our nerve and toy with the idea of running away from it all...

It may be good, if you can, to have a holiday from all the pressures, but it's just plain silly to think we can run away from God. And often, when we're under pressure, we lose the vital perspective that the God who knows us, also loves us with a deep, caring and gentle passion.

⌄ Apply

God knows all there is to know about you—even things you are completely unaware of. But he still has a firm hold on us to lead and protect us... So we can live as his enemy, trying to escape him (stupidity). Or we can trust him in his knowledge and power (security).

⌃ Pray

Read the whole psalm through again as a prayer, as though you'd written it yourself...

Dragon versus woman

In the first eleven chapters of Revelation, the key question is "What do you see?" In chapters 12 – 14, the question changes to "Who do you worship?"

Revelation 12 retells the whole of human history as a drama involving three characters: a woman, a child and a dragon.

Read Revelation 12:1-9

- ❷ *Who might the woman be (v 1-2)? (Hint: There may be more than one answer!)*
- ❷ *Who is the child? (Hint: There is only one answer!)*
- ❷ *Who is the dragon (v 3)? And what is the significance of how he is described?*

The woman could be Mary since she gives birth to Jesus. But she's more likely to be the people of God as a whole. Isaiah portrays Israel as a woman in childbirth, waiting to bring forth the Messiah (Isaiah 26:17; 66:6), and the woman in Revelation spans the whole history of redemption. Revelation 12:17 refers to Christians as "the rest of her offspring"—the product of the mission of the church. The child is Jesus. Verse 5 quotes Psalm 2:9, where God's Messiah receives an iron sceptre to rule the nations. The dragon (Satan) is portrayed as terrifyingly dangerous: strong, clever, with enormous power. The drama unfolds in three acts.

Act One: Jesus comes

Read Revelation 12:4-6

- ❷ *What does the dragon try to do?*
- ❷ *How is he thwarted?*
- ❷ *What incidents in the life of Christ does this story remind you of?*

Verses 1-6 refer to the first coming of Jesus seen as a single event, encompassing his birth, the cross (Satan's attempt to devour the child) and his ascension (the child being snatched up to heaven). Throughout history Satan has opposed God's people, and sought to destroy them.

Act Two: Satan goes

Read Revelation 12:7-9

- ❷ *When does the angelic war take place?*
- ❷ *What is the result?*
- ❷ *What do you think this refers to?*

Job 1 suggests that before the coming of Jesus, Satan had access to heaven, and what he did in heaven was accuse God's people. But he and his angels have now "lost their place in heaven"—that is, Satan can no longer accuse us because God's people are now righteous through the death and resurrection of Jesus. We shouldn't focus on Satan's *location,* for the spatial imagery of being in heaven is used in Revelation 12 metaphorically to describe Satan's power to accuse.

But where does this leave us now?

🔺 Pray

Praise God that the power of Satan has been crushed by the cross of Christ.

Thank God that, in Christ, we have a righteousness that can never be challenged.

We are here

Jesus has come, and Satan has been defeated through the cross and resurrection; but what is happening now?

The church triumphant

Read Revelation 12:10-11

- ❓ *Who is now in charge, according to the voice from heaven (v 10)?*
- ❓ *What can Satan no longer do (v 10)?*
- ❓ *How was and is Satan defeated (v 11)?*
- ❓ *What does this require of Christians?*

The reason Satan can no longer legitimately accuse us is because God's people are now righteous through the death and resurrection of Jesus. Satan is defeated through the cross. The verdict has been given in the court of heaven. The prosecution case against Christians is rejected and the prosecution counsel is silenced. Only the defence counsel remains—Jesus our advocate (Romans 8:34). The defendant is declared not guilty. There is no condemnation (Romans 8:1). The archangel Michael is simply the bailiff carrying out the eviction order that was secured at the cross. If Satan had been victorious, then the saints would have been cast out of heaven because his accusations against us would have been vindicated. But Christ is victorious, so it's Satan who is cast out and we are vindicated in Christ. Satan loses his "place" (Revelation 12:8) because we have gained a place.

But there is another piece to this battle.

The church militant

Read Revelation 12:11-12

- ❓ *What should our response be to all this?*
- ❓ *What is Satan doing now?*

Verse 12 tells us that Satan has been thrown down to earth in a great rage. He is doomed but still dangerous, like a defeated army that is in full retreat and yet doing its best to inflict whatever damage it can on the victors. And the focus is on "the word of … testimony" that is given by God's people. It is the testimony—the gospel—that draws others into Christ's forgiveness. And it is the faithful bearing of that testimony through persecution and suffering that brings the saints, like their Saviour, to heaven at last.

This is why it's so tough to live as a Christian. We are struggling against a defeated but still dangerous dragon.

☑ Apply

- ❓ *How true to your own experience is this picture of the current spiritual reality?*
- ❓ *In what ways do you experience the accusations and hostility of Satan in the course of everyday life?*
- ❓ *How do the death and ascension of Jesus enable us to respond to Satan's attacks?*

Church warfare

We often like to think of our weekly church gathering as a place of peace and quiet, or of joyful family fellowship, or as a place of learning.

But should also be seen as something else: a bloody battlefield?

Act Three: Warfare!

Read Revelation 12:13-17

- ❓ *What stories from the Old Testament does this narrative bring to mind?*
- ❓ *Who is the woman that the dragon pursues?*
- ❓ *How would this story help and encourage Christians who are suffering persecution?*

The woman flees to the wilderness (v 14), just as Elijah did from Jezebel and Jesus fled to Egypt from Herod. But the imagery of Act Three is primarily drawn from the exodus. The church is experiencing a second exodus. In Exodus 19:4, at Mount Sinai, God says of Israel, "You yourselves have seen what I did to Egypt, and how I carried you on eagles' wings and brought you to myself". Now again God is rescuing his people on eagles' wings. The flood is a common image in the Old Testament for overwhelming evil (Psalm 18:4; Isaiah 43:2). Now God keeps his people for a symbolic 42 months before they inherit the promised new creation (Revelation 12:14).

God's people are a wilderness people, not at home in a hostile world. But in the wilderness we are nourished and kept by God, just as Israel was nourished by manna and protected by the pillars of cloud and fire.

⌄ Apply

John portrays the struggle of the church as a great cosmic battle, spanning heaven and earth. This is an epic *Lord-of-the-Rings* or *Narnia*-type narrative. He locates the struggle of his readers in the biggest possible context. Their day-to-day struggle to live without compromise is part of a battle that touches heaven itself. In verse 1 the church is viewed from the perspective of heaven, and she is glorious and reigning over the universe: "A great sign appeared in heaven: a woman clothed with the sun, with the moon under her feet, and a crown of twelve stars on her head". Despite all that we may suffer, this is a description of you *now*.

The chapter reminds us that Satan is both a real *and* a defeated foe. The one command in the chapter is in verse 12: *Rejoice!* Both truths should motivate us. There is no place for apathy, and there is no need for despair.

⌃ Pray

If Satan is accusing you, rejoice that Christ's blood is all you need.

If you are facing Satan's hostility, ask the Lord for the strength to love him and the gospel more than your life.

And pray for your brothers and sisters in parts of the world where being a faithful witness can lead to physical harm and death.

The power of the beast

In Revelation 13 we see the current manifestation of Satan's influence, as two beasts appear who dominate the world and persecute God's people.

Once again, we need to understand that John is not describing a *sequence* of events, but piling up pictures on top of each other to engage our imaginations and locate our current experiences in the cosmic drama. *It's a bit like this; or it's a bit like that...*

Read Revelation 13:1-4

- ❓ *What do you think the first beast represents, from its description?*
- ❓ *How does the beast exercise its power?*
- ❓ *How does the world respond to the beast (v 4)?*

The first beast represents the political and military power of empire. In John's time, this was the arrival of Roman armies across the Mediterranean to conquer Asia Minor. Its ten horns, seven heads and ten crowns are a reworking of the images in Daniel 7, in which Daniel sees successive empires. Here is the latest expression of imperial power. It looks like various fierce carnivores—animals used by Rome to signify its power.

☑ Apply

Worship doesn't always look religious. The people admire the strength and achievements of the beast, in the same way that people today might take great pride in our military, or in the achievements of science, or in our sporting prowess. We feel strong and successful because our team or nation is. We place ultimate value (worship) where it does not belong.

Beast talk

Read Revelation 13:5-10

- ❓ *What do we learn about the character and motivation of the beast?*
- ❓ *What is encouraging about verse 7?*
- ❓ *How are we meant to understand verses 9-10?*

Although these verses were clearly written about the Roman empire at the time, the beast could be *any* empire throughout history. Not all power is bad and not all empires are evil. But this empire utters "blasphemies" (v 5-6). It takes the place of God, redefines morality and demands ultimate allegiance (v 8). Inevitably that brings it into conflict with God's people, for we have a competing allegiance. So it wages war against the church (v 7). The results are inevitable: Christians will be imprisoned and martyred (v 9-10). It's not hard to find parallels of this today: North Korea is one. In the West we don't live under an idolatrous empire. But there are idolatrous elements to our society. Our governments are redefining morality in areas like euthanasia, abortion, gender and sexuality. We too live under the influence of the beast.

☑ Apply

The beast has no power of its own, but only what is given to it (v 7). We can be confident that whatever is happening, it is God who is ultimately in control.

The second beast

We may not live under an oppressive domineering government that demands our absolute obedience. Perhaps it is the second beast we should be more fearful of...

Innocent?

Read Revelation 13:11-17

❓ *What is confusing about the description in verse 11?*

❓ *How does the second beast secure its following (v 12-14)?*

❓ *Who does it serve, and what is its ultimate aim?*

The second beast looks like a lamb—innocent and harmless in a twisted parody of Jesus. But it speaks the words of the dragon, Satan. The second beast is the propagandist. It's not providing a reasoned case for empire. It produces signs and images to seduce, threaten, impress and overwhelm the peoples of the earth (v 13-15).

The Roman Empire exercised control not only through military power but also through access to its prosperity. "Soft power", we would call it today, or "winning hearts and minds". The point is not to look for literal marks today (like barcodes). The point is that the beast demands our allegiance. It uses both carrot and stick: acquiesce and you can share in the bounty; resist and you're excluded. This isn't just state power; it can also be peer pressure.

✓ Apply

John invites us to question the propaganda of the second beast and see through its images. All its wonders are a parody of God. It makes fire come down from heaven (v 13), as Elijah did (1 Kings 18). It performs signs and wonders (Revelation 13:14), just as Jesus and the apostles did. It exalts the beast who was wounded and yet lives, just as Christians exalt the Lamb who was slain but rose again. The triumvirate of the dragon and the two beasts form a parody of the Trinity. Through a thousand adverts and glossy magazines, the beast says, *All this could be yours if you bow before me.* John wants us to see the work of the second beast for what it is. He wants us to reject its seductions and worship Christ instead.

❓ *What aspects of modern life would you find hardest to lose?*

❓ *Do you recognise the subtle pressure this places on us to conform?*

Numbered

Read Revelation 13:18

❓ *What do you think this number means?*

There are many theories: one is that 666 is the sum of Nero's name in a Hebrew system in which letters were assigned numeric values. If so, John is saying the wise person realises Nero and his successors are the latest manifestation of satanic power. Alternatively, it may represent one less than the perfection represented by 777. If so, John is saying that the wise person recognises imperial power is not good, nor the final word in history.

The numbered saints

After the horrific visions of the last two chapters, John now looks and sees an alternative vision.

Sealed

Read Revelation 14:1-5

- ❷ *What is the significance of the mark (compare 13:16-17)?*
- ❷ *What is the significance of the number of people?*
- ❷ *Make a list of the qualities that lead to inclusion in this musical multitude.*
- ❷ *What do you think verse 4 means?*

John sees Jesus, the Lamb, surrounded by 144,000, representing all God's true people. The second beast put a mark on people giving them access to the market and the glories of Rome. The 144,000 have the marks of the Lamb and the Father, indicating their inclusion in the glories of his kingdom.

Throughout Revelation, immorality is a picture of spiritual adultery. So, again, these are not literal sexual virgins—but those who have kept themselves free of the seductions of empire. And what do they do? They sing (Revelation 14:2-3). While the world worships the beast, they worship the Lamb.

···· TIME OUT ····

Jehovah's Witnesses claim that this number is a real, literal number, and that the 144,000 are a special subset of believers.

- ❷ *How might you challenge this claim in a doorstep conversation in a way that leads towards the gospel?*

Saints

Read Revelation 14:1-5 again

- ❷ *Look again at the qualities that mark those who have been sealed. How can these be true for us?*
- ❷ *How does that make you feel?*

Who can claim that they are undefiled, follow the Lamb wherever he goes, have never lied, and are blameless? If you belong to Jesus—*you can!*

We have received the righteousness of Christ, and the Father accepts us as having all the love, faithfulness and purity of his Son, Jesus. The challenge for us is to live out that new, true identity, rather than slip back into our old ways of thinking and living. In that direction there is only death and judgment. With Christ there is joy and life. But victory only comes through suffering.

☑ Apply

- ❷ *Which of these qualities do you most struggle to live up to in your daily life?*
- ❷ *In what area do you think our culture most puts pressure on us to conform?*

Pray that you, your church, and God's people throughout the world would live with the clarity this vision presents; and strive to live joyfully and truthfully as we worship Jesus.

Double trouble

Trouble comes in a number of forms. There's the one-off crisis—knocking us down when we least expect it. And there is the steady, relentless grind of insoluble difficulties that dog our steps for years.

❓ *Do you cope differently with these stresses? Which would you prefer to have?*

Hard times can easily detach us from God. Psalms 140 – 143 will show us how David coped with wave after wave of agony.

Slandered

Read Psalm 140:1-5

❓ *What is David's first reaction to trouble?*

It's a mark of the genuine believer. Some people pick up the phone and complain to their friends, some just run away. Others turn to the bottle or pills. The Christian instinct is to turn first to God.

···· **TIME OUT** ····································

Tea and sympathy with Christian friends can have great restorative value (beware of the gossip factor, however). And sometimes it's right to seek medical advice for help. But David's instinct is surely right. Turn to God and pray.

❓ *Is this your reaction when trouble lands on your doorstep? If not, how can you cultivate that prayerful response?*

What to pray for

Read Psalm 140:6-13

❓ *What does David pray for himself (v 1-5)?*

❓ *And what does he pray for those who slander him (v 8-11)?*

❓ *List the truths about God that he hangs onto in verses 6-7, 12-13. We counted at least seven; maybe you can find more...*

-
-
-
-
-
-
-
-

❓ *And how does this knowledge of God's character, ability and past deeds help David (see v 12-13)?*

⌃ Pray

Turn the list above into praise and prayer, asking God (who is your God) to help you remember correctly, and respond rightly, in times of crisis.

Three angels

How much does it matter if people believe in Jesus? Our culture wants to make all choices valid, but there are three angels that want us to think again...

Read Revelation 14:6-11

❓ *What message does the first angel give, and to whom?*
❓ *What about the second angel?*
❓ *And the third?*
❓ *What is the stark decision that is placed before humankind?*

The angels are all representing some aspect of gospel preaching. The first sends out to the whole world the call to worship the one true God. The second prophetically preaches to the culture, exposing the bankruptcy of any kingdom other than the kingdom of Christ. The third shows the awful seriousness of choosing which side you align with. At Martin Luther's funeral, his friend Johann Bugenhagen, preaching from verse 6, identified Luther as the first angel. It would be wrong to suggest John exclusively had Luther in mind when he wrote this, but he did have people *like* Luther in mind. As gospel preachers, we must embrace aspects of all three of these angelic themes in our message to others.

⌄ Apply

❓ *Which of these messages do you find easiest to articulate?*
❓ *Which of them do you find most difficult?*
❓ *How can you encourage yourself, and others, to embrace and articulate these messages in your conversations with others?*

Rest and retribution
Read Revelation 14:9-13

❓ *What will happen to those who worship the beast (v 9-11)?*
❓ *What will happen to those who worship the Lord?*
❓ *What does John encourage us to focus on in verse 12?*

The contrast is stark. *Everybody dies*, but the destiny of each is determined by who you worship in this life. Worshipping the beast ends in judgment and torment. Worshipping the Lamb leads to rest and blessing in the next life. John focuses our minds on the things that really matter: remaining faithful and obedient, and having patience to ride out whatever temporary suffering we have to endure—either personal or from persecution inflicted by the state.

⌃ Pray

Pray for those you know—family, friends, neighbours—whose worship is directed towards something other than Jesus Christ.

Pray that they would understand the seriousness of where this will lead them.

Pray that you would be a faithful, obedient witness to them.

Pray for an opportunity to share the message of the angels with others today.

Two harvests

The Lord Jesus told many parables in which the harvest was a picture of God's final judgment. John spells it out for us in arresting detail.

Sharp sickles

Read Revelation 14:14-20

❓ *Who is doing the harvesting (v 14)?*
❓ *When does the harvest happen (v 15)?*
❓ *What does the harvest of the grapes symbolise?*

The image of harvesting is rich with meaning. It gathers in the good fruit of course. But in Jesus' parables, it also is the moment when any false plants (e.g. weeds) are uprooted and destroyed. This might be reflected here if the first wheat harvest is the gathering of the godly; or there may simply be an emphasis that the judgment *will* take place when everything is good and ready.

The grape harvest is crushed in a winepress, and blood flows out 2 metres deep in a river 200 miles long—the length of the Thames in England or the Suwannee in Florida. The point is clear: judgment will be swift, decisive, complete, overwhelming.

Again the choice facing John's readers—then and now—is presented in the starkest terms. The core issue is: who or what do you worship? The "world" is not just a different lifestyle or philosophy. It's a different worship system. Economics and politics matter because they're an expression of your ultimate allegiance. This section is peppered with exhortations to remain faithful in the face of imperial seduction and threats (12:11; 13:10; 14:12-13).

✔ Apply

At many times in the past, and now in the present, there have been oppressive governments that demand the worship of their citizens, and imprison, suppress, torture and kill those who dare to defy them.

But is there is a more subtle version of this in our own world that similarly demands our allegiance? Currently, we are not controlled by baton-wielding police on the street corners. But we are increasingly being controlled by the corporations that know all about us, who are increasingly able to manipulate us into buying and being what they want.

❓ *What might "subversive worship" look like in our internet- and media-dominated age?*

▲ Pray

Judgment is coming. It will be swift, decisive, complete and overwhelming.

Pray that the gospel message would reach your friends, family, neighbours and community before the harvest is ripe, and it is too late.

Look up the words to *The Battle Hymn of the Republic,* which is partly based on this passage. Use its stirring, triumphant ideas to fuel your prayer and praise.

The song of the Lamb

We have singing in heaven a number of times already in Revelation. Now John picks up another song as the conflicts of the last chapters come to an end.

In 7:9-10 a great multitude sings of a heavenly throne. In 11:15 heaven sings of an exalted Lord with the power to spin destinies and bestow kingdoms. Let's listen in to this new song:

Read Revelation 15:1-4

❷ *What is the description of heaven in verse 2 meant to convey?*

❷ *Who does John see in heaven? What have they had to do to get there?*

❷ *What is the theme of their song, and why is that important?*

The description of heaven is certainly otherworldly. Glass is a mundane material to us, but in the ancient world glass was a rare and valuable commodity. To have a floor the size of a sea to walk upon was unimaginable. John wants to give us an overwhelming sense of the glory, beauty and wealth of eternity, in contrast to which the visible splendour of the Roman Empire pales by comparison.

The harp-plucking singers are those who have remained faithful to God and so have won victory over the beast (v 2). But the song makes it clear whose victory this really is. It is not a victory won by our work and endurance. It is God alone who is holy. It is God alone to whom the glory belongs. This victory is not by works, but by the gracious work of God.

···· TIME OUT ····

Read Exodus 15:1-18

The song in Revelation deliberately picks up echoes of the song of Moses after another evil empire that had oppressed and threatened the people of God was defeated—Egypt. By making these connections, John is reminding us that the history of God's people has been a repeated experience of God's saving power over the forces that threaten to overwhelm us. However dark things look now, if we are in Christ, we can be confident that the victory will be ours in the end.

⌄ Apply

Christian worship is always a subversive act, akin to singing the French national anthem in occupied France during World War Two. In our corporate worship we call one another both *to* the worship of the true God and *from* the worship of other gods. We call one another from the subtle influence of the empty and destructive idolatries of this world. Instead, we give our undivided allegiance to the one, undivided God.

❷ *How can we ensure that our worship is truly an act of defiance against the idolatrous claims of the world?*

Completing wrath

We love detective dramas because the crook is always caught and justice is always done. But life is darker than that. In the real world, by and large, evil triumphs…

But the book of Revelation offers us an alternative ending. Revelation chapters 4 – 11 offered hope for those longing for security in an insecure world. Chapters 15 – 16 offer hope for those longing for justice in an unjust world. And this hope is not a fiction.

The seven bowls

Read Revelation 15:5-8

- ❓ *What does the imagery in this section remind you of elsewhere in the Bible?*
- ❓ *What happens in these verses? What feeling does this scene convey to you?*
- ❓ *What is in the bowls?*
- ❓ *What do you think the heavenly temple represents?*
- ❓ *What encouragement is there in verses 1 and 8 that there is an end in sight?*

Another cycle of seven begins—seven bowls with seven plagues. But this cycle is climatic because with them "God's wrath is completed" (v 1). The bowls are introduced by God's people (v 2), singing in praise of God's justice (v 3-4). They stand beside a sea of glass (v 2). The sea symbolised chaos and threat in the Hebrew worldview. So a sea of glass is a sign that God is about to calm the forces of evil.

In the drama of Revelation, the bowls come from the temple in heaven, which John calls "the tabernacle of the covenant law" (v 5). God's judgment is not arbitrary but based on his revealed will (his "covenant law").

The angels who will deliver the judgments of the seven bowls are dressed like Christ, for they are his representatives (v 6; see 1:13). The divine origin of these judgment is reinforced in 15:8, where the smoke of God's glory fills the temple. Even the holy angels cannot enter God's presence (v 8), far less unholy humanity. The lightning, thunder and earthquake of 16:18 recall Mount Sinai (Exodus 19:16-18), but this time God has come down to judge. The end is in sight, but we are told that this is the last thing to happen before sinful people can enter the heavenly temple. Just as seeing the finishing line helps a runner sustain themselves for the last lap, so seeing the prize clearly will help John's readers, and us, remain faithful to the end, even as the bowls are poured out.

TIME OUT

If you have time, read some of the Old Testament stories that are referenced here. John's first readers would know these images, and know what he was talking about.

Read Isaiah 6:1-4; 51:17, 22; Exodus 40:34-35; 1 Kings 8:10-11

🔼 Pray

Ask the Lord to help you fix your eyes on the finish line: heaven, eternity, the new creation. Pray that this vision would sustain you through all you will face in the future.

The bowls of wrath

We reach the last cycle of "sevens": following from the seals, the trumpet, and the thunders—which were mercifully cancelled before they were enacted.

But there is something different about the bowls...

The first three bowls

Read Revelation 16:1-7

❷ *What do these bowls remind you of? Why is that significant, do you think?*

❷ *What does each of them do? Why are these things so frightening?*

❷ *Who is affected by them (v 2)?*

❷ *What is different about those the bowls affect, compared with the trumpets and the seals (compare v 3 with 6:8 and 8:7)?*

❷ *What is different about the purpose of the bowls (compare 15:1 with 9:20-21)?*

The seals affect one in four (6:8) and the trumpets affect one in three (8:7). The seven thunders, had they not been rescinded (10:3-4), would presumably have affected one in two. But the bowls affect one in one: *everyone* and *everything* (16:3). The bowls have their effect on everyone who worships the beast: those who live in the kingdom of this world, not the kingdom of Jesus.

But these is also a finality about these plagues. The seals and trumpets included a call to repentance (9:20-21), but the bowls are signs of final judgment "because with them God's wrath is completed" (15:1). The seven bowls are no longer *educative*. They are *retributive*. They have a different function: to establish and complete the justice of God.

····· TIME OUT ·····

These plagues remind us of the plagues of Egypt, where God dealt with another oppressive power that threatened his people. That cycle of ten plagues ended in the final liberation of his people and the defeat of the enemy. John's point is clear: what God did *then*, he will do *again* for you as you labour under the harsh oppression of a pagan state, intent on enslaving you.

The reason for wrath

Read Revelation 16:5-7 again

❷ *What reasons does the angel give for the horrors poured out from the bowls?*

❷ *As horrific as they are, why are these judgments "true and just" (v 7)?*

❷ *How does this help us as we think about God's judgment on individuals and the world?*

⌄ Apply

Many today are shocked by the idea that God will judge people. Sometimes we feel the same thing: *Will God really send people to hell? Surely what they have done is not that bad.*

❷ *What would John (and the angels) have to say in response to this?*

❷ *How might you answer someone who expresses their shock at the finality of God's future judgment?*

Shaking the earth

The first three bowls produced horrific effects on the earth and sea. But these last four bowls shake the very foundations of the cosmos…

Wrong responses

Read Revelation 16:8-11

- ❷ *What happens with these two plagues?*
- ❷ *What is the response of the people to their situation?*
- ❷ *What does this remind you of from the Old Testament?*
- ❷ *What is so fitting about the judgment poured out with the fifth bowl?*

Job was covered in sores, and yet he refused to curse God (Job 2:9-11). Pharaoh faced mounting pressure from the plagues, and yet he continually "hardened his heart" (Exodus 8:32). The responses to the fourth and fifth bowls make it clear which side people are on. They blaspheme God—the only one with the power to save them—and do not repent or give him glory. Under the same circumstances, the righteous person, like Job, would take a different path.

Darkness is a fitting end to the kingdom that loved darkness rather than light. Loving darkness results in self-loathing and misery, but still these people would rather cling onto what little they think they have than turn and trust God.

The sixth bowl

Read Revelation 16:12-16

- ❷ *What does the drying of the Euphrates make possible (v 12)?*
- ❷ *What are the dragon, the beast and the false prophet ultimately revealed to be?*

- ❷ *What is important for Christians to focus on as all this is happening (v 15)?*

The drying up of the River Euphrates in verse 12 recalls the exodus story, when God delivered his people by drying a path through the Red Sea before destroying the Egyptian army. But it also recalls Cyrus, who, as promised by Isaiah 44:27-28, destroyed historical Babylon by diverting the river. These horrors are not meant to terrify those who belong to Jesus. We are meant to be watchful, ensuring that when Christ returns to judge the world, we are found faithful.

The seventh bowl

Read Revelation 16:17-21

- ❷ *What are we meant to feel as the seventh bowl is poured out?*
- ❷ *What indications are there that this is the end?*
- ❷ *How do the people respond to this last plague?*

Unlike the other "sevens", there is no pause before the last bowl. This is it. It is done. And yet, even in the face of these supernatural events, the people are unable to repent, and instead curse God.

⌃ Pray

Ask that God would have mercy and give the grace to repent to those without Christ.

Trouble and strife

It's crisis time for David again. But this time he responds with a series of strange requests.

Provoked...

Read Psalm 141

❷ *How desperate is David (v 1, 2)?*
❷ *But, strangely, what is he chiefly concerned about?*

Curiously, in the face of great provocation, he pleads with God for self-control. He is desperate not to retaliate with vicious words (v 3), or to get involved in his opponents' tactics (v 4)—but only to be remembered for speaking with gracious words (v 6). He is even prepared to take fair criticism (v 5)!

✓ Apply

So, let's admit it. Despite the calm exterior, we're often boiling with rage inside, thinking about how we're going to "get back at them" or imagining cruel and unusual punishments for those who rub us up the wrong way. If you're anything like me, then you are particularly vulnerable to this kind of thinking when you are behind the wheel of the car.

❷ *Perhaps it's time to take a leaf from David's book, and pray the words of verses 3-5...*

... but protected

❷ *Why is it that David can behave so sensibly, humbly and spiritually, when his bones are crying out for revenge?*
❷ *Do you see the answers in verses 6-8?*

TIME OUT

Although this psalm was written by David, it is also the song of great David's greater son, who supremely showed self-control before his false accusers—and entrusted himself, life, body and soul to the One who could vindicate him.

Compare Luke 23:8,9 with Psalm 141:3-4; and Luke 23:47 with Psalm 141:6b.

✓ Apply

David had learned to leave judgment in the hands of the one just Judge, trusting that he would vindicate him. And he cried out to God for the strength to remain godly, even as he was being persecuted.

❷ *Is that a lesson you have learned?*
❷ *Is that a prayer you will pray now?*

Where is your home?

The final chapters of the book of Revelation describe two cities, both of which are likened to women: Babylon the prostitute and Jerusalem the bride.

They represent two communities, two sets of values, two futures. And the question John poses to us is: Where do you belong? Are you seduced by the treasures of this earth or is your heart set on heavenly treasure? Do you feel at home in the world or do you belong to the empire of the Lamb?

The scarlet woman

Read Revelation 17:1-6

- ❓ *What conflicting images of the woman do we see in these verses?*
- ❓ *What clues are there in the passage to what these figures of the beast and the woman represent?*
- ❓ *What does the mark on her forehead reveal about her?*
- ❓ *How does this new vision match up with what has come before in Revelation?*

The world of Revelation was a world of cities, as today's world is for us. And cities were often personified as women. Rome was personified as the goddess Roma, and this is how she was worshipped in Asia Minor, where John's readers live. But in Revelation, she appears not as a goddess, but as a prostitute (v 1) who seduces the world, drawing people into her idolatry (v 2). The fact that John is introduced to her by one of the angels who had one of the bowls suggests that we are about to see the reason for God's wrath. Babylon persecutes God's people (v 6). She is the manifestation of the power of the dragon, the beast and the prophet (v 3). A name or mark on the forehead in Revelation indicates a person's true character, and hers is clear. She is "the Mother of Prostitutes" because her children (her inhabitants) share her spiritual adultery.

⌄ Apply

Babylon, like Babel before her, is symbolic of the city that sets itself in opposition to God. Oppressive regimes like Babylon create empires that persecute any who dare to think or live differently. The images in this passage seem stark, bloody, ugly. It is easy to see the similarity with totalitarian regimes in history or in our own day. And yet, to some extent, they describe the cities and empires we live in.

- ❓ *What signs do you see that your own culture behaves like a gaudy prostitute that entices people in and consumes them?*
- ❓ *What might it look like for Christians to resist her charms?*

⌃ Pray

Ask God to give you eyes to see the reality of the culture in which we live, and wisdom to know what genuine faithfulness looks like.

The resilient beast

As we read chapter 17, we need to remember what John is doing. He is using layers of different imaginative images to tell us the same thing over and over again.

Astonished
Read Revelation 17:6-8

❷ *Why might John be astonished (or "marvel", v 6, ESV) at this vision?*

❷ *If the beast (or Babylon) that John is referring to is Rome, and any oppressive regime set against God, what do you think the phrase "once was, now is not, and yet will come" refers to (v 7)?*

❷ *What becomes of the beast in the end?*

❷ *Why do you think those who are not saved (v 8) are also astonished?*

John, it seems, is astonished by this vision, probably in dread, though possibly with attraction—we have already noted the dissonance in this image: a beautiful, bejewelled, beguiling woman with ruthless bloody intent. But John's angelic guide will expose her false glory. Think of John's description of Babylon the prostitute in terms of a political cartoonist, presenting an exaggerated and outlandish personification of the city to satirise her pompous claims. Think of a bloated Britannia or Uncle Sam squashing the British lion or American eagle upon which they sit. This is the kind of imagery that John is evoking in this powerful word picture.

Twice in Revelation 17:7-8 we're told that the beast "once was, now is not, and yet will come". In other words, the beast manifests itself in one form. This then passes away and "is not". Throughout history the beast returns in other guises. This phrase is another parody of the living God, "who is, and who was, and who is to come" (1:8; 4:8; 11:16; 16:5). The Roman empire was one of a long line of many others. But it fell, and new empires arose, including ours.

✔ Apply

Our world is truly astonishing. Its achievements are immense, its technology miraculous, its abilities seemingly endless, its wealth staggering. No wonder we are so easily beguiled by the bright lights and enjoyments it offers. But understanding this vision will expose the crucial difference between the astonishment of the faithful saints and the astonishment of those who have not had their names written in the book of life from before the creation of the world. We recognise that the world is, at the end of the day, a prostitute whose calls we must resist. There is only one destiny for those who follow her. We fix our eyes on a different prize.

❷ *What do you find most attractive and enjoyable about the modern world we live in?*

❷ *How can you enjoy these blessings without being consumed by them?*

❷ *How can you remind yourself day by day, moment by moment, that we walk to the beat of a different drum?*

The mystery revealed

"This calls for a mind of wisdom" (v 9). As we draw to the end of this section of Revelation, pray that God would give you wise understanding of these difficult verses.

Read Revelation 17:9-18

- ❓ *What are the giveaway clues that John is referring to Rome in these verses?*
- ❓ *What do the kings and the beast want to do (v 14)?*
- ❓ *What happens to the prostitute in the end (v 16)?*
- ❓ *Who is in charge of all this, and for what purpose (v 17)?*

In 17:10-12 the angel speaks of coming kings and transfers of power. The details may be confusing to us, but if we step back, the bigger picture is clear. In Daniel 7 the same language is used to describe successive empires. So the symbolic numbers seven and ten in Revelation 17:3 and verses 10-12 probably don't refer to specific kings. Instead John is highlighting the way the beast manifests its power in recurring political empires and systems throughout history. For example, Domitian (probably the emperor when John was writing) was regarded as a second Nero. So these chapters speak simultaneously to the specific situation of first-century Rome and to every age.

⌄ Apply

- ❓ *What are you tempted to think when you react to news of major world events: powers overthrown, coups d'etat, revolutions?*
- ❓ *How does John want us to react (v 17)?*

Poetic justice

Read Revelation 17:15-17 again

- ❓ *What is ironic about the way the woman is ruined?*
- ❓ *How do we see this principle at work in our world today?*

Though the woman "rides" on the beast and "rules" over kings (v 7, 18), in verse 16 they turn on her and destroy her. The city of Rome will be destroyed by the very empire it built-in fulfilment of God's word of judgment (v 17). The allegiance of Rome's client rulers is an act of self-interest and, when the political climate shifts, they will be quick to switch that allegiance. This is precisely what happened in AD 410, when Rome was sacked by people it had once ruled.

Or John may have in mind a closer event. Domitian's cruelty made him a figure of hatred, and when he was assassinated in AD 96, people across the empire celebrated by smashing his statues.

⌃ Pray

Paul says in Romans 1 that God's wrath is being revealed by the way he gives people up to their own ways—and allows them to suffer the consequences.

Pray that the Lord would have mercy on our lost world, and that we would remain faithful witnesses—whatever our circumstances.

ACTS: The journey begins

We are returning to the book of Acts and entering a phase of the book which centres upon the missionary journeys of the apostle Paul.

In Antioch
Read Acts 12:25 – 13:3

Luke includes the details of 13:1 to indicate the growing influence of Antioch as a hub of Christian activity. He portrays Antioch as an equal to Jerusalem in terms of influence in the Christian world.

> ❓ *What was the church doing, and what happened while they did that (v 2)?*

Churches today settle for a watered-down vision of fellowship which typically includes eating a meal, and talking about the newest movies and latest professional sport developments. But true fellowship radiates the glories of Christ through prayer and love. At this prayer meeting in Antioch, God spoke and set apart two men who would turn the world upside down. Never underestimate the power of true fellowship when God's people gather together in prayer.

> ❓ *How does the church respond to the Spirit's leading (v 3)?*

☑ Apply

> ❓ *In what ways do you and your church experience the kind of fellowship we see in these verses? What might need to change?*

From Antioch
Read Acts 13:4-12

···· TIME OUT ····

The "John" in verse 5 is John Mark, the author of the Gospel of Mark. Saul and Barnabas would have had no indication that God would use him as an inspired New Testament author. Every glorious end has humble beginnings.

Paul, Saul and John reach the Cypriot town of Paphos (v 6).

> ❓ *Who is Bar-Jesus, and what is his aim (v 6, 8)?*
> ❓ *Who is Sergius Paulus, and what is his aim (v 7)?*
> ❓ *What is the result of Saul's intervention (v 11-12)?*

The magician begins to oppose them by influencing the proconsul away from the message of the gospel. This sort of anti-missionary effort will span the rest of the narrative of Acts. This does not, however, deter Paul and Barnabas from proclaiming the good news. No amount of persecution or rejection will hinder their zeal for gospel proclamation. Nor will it prevent people from turning to Christ in faith as the apostles teach (v 12).

☐ Pray

Ask God to give you the same confidence in the gospel that this missionary team had, so that you would teach the gospel clearly even when there is opposition.

You need Jesus

As Paul reaches Pisidian Antioch in Galatia, we get to listen to his gospel preaching for the first time. Luke has already included some of Peter's sermons—here's one of Paul's.

Read Acts 13:13-41

Notice the detail in verse 16, before Paul starts speaking. It's the same as Peter did in 12:17. Luke includes these details in order to parallel Peter and Paul as the two key apostolic preachers of the first-century church.

The God of Israel

❓ *To whom is Paul speaking (13:16)?*
❓ *What does he remind them about:*
   • *what God had done (v 17-22a)?*
   • *what God had promised (v 22)?*
❓ *What does Paul then claim (v 23, 32-33)?*

Paul recounts the death, burial and resurrection of Jesus Christ. For Paul, these events brought to fruition the entire redemptive plan of God in the Scriptures and secured the good news of eternal salvation. Paul reveals how all of God's word points to the coming Christ and the ministry of Jesus.

Jesus the Messiah

❓ *What does Paul want his audience to know (v 38-39)?*

Remember his audience: Jews who thought salvation came through works of the law. The Bible teaches the inability of the law to save (see Galatians 2:16; Romans 3:20). The law could not save because of the power of sin. The law does not provide salvation but points to the need for salvation. Salvation comes not by works but by faith in the one who fulfilled the law's demands perfectly.

❓ *What does Paul want his audience to beware (Acts 13:40-41)?*

There is no such thing as a neutral response to the gospel. The gospel demands repentance and faith in Jesus Christ; anything less amounts to a rejection of God's grace and provision through the cross of his Son.

We can learn from Paul's style of presentation. On the one hand, he exuded empathy as he grounded his message in something familiar to his audience that they would have understood (v 16-22). But Paul then advanced his message to the uniqueness of Christ, which would have required courage and conviction. We need both empathy and courage in order to present the gospel effectively, persuasively and passionately.

⌄ Apply

Think about the kinds of people you live near and have the opportunity to share the gospel with.

❓ *What would it look like to explain it to them in a way that is both empathetic and courageous?*
❓ *Do you think you tend to lack empathy, or courage, in your gospel witness?*

Advancing and suffering

Paul has invited his hearers to find forgiveness in Christ and warned them to beware rejecting him. So, how will Pisidian Antioch respond to the arrival of the gospel?

Read Acts 13:42-44

❓ *What kinds of response do Paul and Barnabas meet with first?*

Read Acts 13:45

❓ *What response does the initial positive response provoke?*

Read Acts 13:46-52

❓ *How do we see those two responses side by side through these verses?*

❓ *How do Paul and Barnabas react to the rejection and accusations of the Jewish leaders (v 46-47, 51)?*

Verse 46 records a massive missiological shift—a watershed moment in the Acts narrative. The gospel will advance to the Gentile world, and Paul now becomes the apostle to the Gentiles.

As it has happened so often in the history of the church, so it is here: great spiritual advancement meets an equally great spiritual hostility. In this case, the influential Jews drive out Paul and Barnabas from the entire district. Paul and Barnabas, however, "shook off the dust off their feet as a warning to them and went to Iconium" (v 51). To shake the dust off your feet was an act of protest and a physical demonstration of disgust.

Paul's actions in Acts 13 indicate that sometimes in our gospel ministry, we might have to shake the dust off our feet and move on to other people. Yet later in Acts, Paul will preach in certain regions where he meets

a more potent hostility than we see here. When, then, should you "shake the dust off your feet"? That is a question between you and the Spirit of God. Sometimes we are led to continue; but sometimes it is wisest to focus our evangelistic efforts elsewhere.

❓ *How do Paul and Barnabas feel about all that has happened to them (v 52)?*

We might find it difficult to count it a joy when faithful living provokes persecution. The Bible, however, reveals how God uses the suffering of his people to accomplish glorious purposes. As Paul says in Colossians 1:24, "Now I rejoice in what I am suffering for you, and I fill up in my flesh what is still lacking in regard to Christ's afflictions, for the sake of his body, which is the church." Paul knew that his suffering joined together with the sufferings of Christ to advance the gospel. That is why he could live joyfully in the midst of suffering for Christ. So can and so should we.

✔ Apply

The opposition to Paul did not make him stop witnessing, but rather led him to witness to different people.

❓ *How do you respond to opposition? Let it not be by giving up altogether.*

❓ *How do you respond to suffering for your faith? Let it be with the joy that Paul knew.*

Dave's cave

This psalm was written before David became king. At this point he was hiding out, on the run from Saul. Saul had realised that David would be king in his place one day.

Saul, wild with jealousy, tried to kill David—hence David's rocky hideout.

Abandoned

Read Psalm 142

❓ *How was David feeling (v 1-4)?*

Distress and loneliness (you've been abandoned, nobody cares about you or understands the trouble you're in) are normal reactions to have in times of trouble. These feelings are not wrong, but what they lead to could be...

❓ *But what was David's reaction in his dire distress (v 2)?*
❓ *How is this an example to you when times are tough?*
❓ *How do you tend to react instead?*

Notice what gives David his great confidence (v 3a).

❓ *What else do we learn about David's situation (v 3b-4)?*
❓ *What did he tell God (v 5)?*

He knew he was abandoned by others (worse, opposed by them)—but not abandoned by God. He knew God was both his "refuge" (a place to escape to for safety) and his "portion" (his satisfaction).

How do you feel?

❓ *Did David bottle up his emotions (v 6)?*
❓ *What did David admit about himself?*
❓ *Why did David want to be rescued (v 7)?*
❓ *Why was he sure he would be?*

By the time he had finished his prayer session, David was full of assurance. He knew God could work deliverance and restore freedom, thankfulness and the opportunity for him to meet God's people again.

⌄ Apply

In *Explore* we tend to focus on applying these psalms to ourselves. This time, let's think about how we can apply it to *others*.

You're drinking coffee after church and chatting with people. In response to the "How are you?" you get the usual "Oh, fine thanks". But something tells you that that's not all there is to tell.

❓ *How would you take the conversation further?*
❓ *From this psalm, what would you encourage your friend to do?*

Don't worship me

The stage is now set: the missionary group will tour the province, promoting the gospel; and the Jewish leaders will follow them, opposing it.

A city divided

Read Acts 14:1-7

❓ *How do we see both acceptance of the gospel and resistance to it in these verses?*

❓ *What is impressive about the response of the "apostles" in verse 7?*

Paul the divine?

Read Acts 14:8-18

❓ *How do the crowds respond to the healing of a lame man (v 11-13)?*

❓ *What does Paul do to attempt to dissuade them from this view (v 14-17)?*

Put simply, the crowds have confused the messenger with the message. And Paul could not let that happen. When someone tore their robe, they did so as an act of abject humiliation and grief. Paul knew that when the crowds confused the messenger with the message, they distorted the entire gospel.

❓ *What does he tell them to do (v 15)?*

Notice the contrasting elements Paul presents: on the one hand, worthless things, and on the other, the living and eternal God. This simple distinction highlights the unsearchable depth of our hardness of heart. Our affections drive us to the created rather than to the Creator. They lead us to worship all kinds of things but not to worship the God who made us and provides for us (v 17).

Paul dismisses their pagan worship, sends the priest of Zeus away, deflects their attempt to honour him as a god, and points them to the one, true God, who did in fact create the world and has continually provided for them through the rain and bountiful harvest seasons. Paul urges them to come and know this living God personally—to forsake worthless things and revel in the resplendent riches of God and his glory.

Even so, the crowds still wish to sacrifice to him (v 18). You can preach your heart out but you cannot raise the dead to life. Only the living God can do that.

✔ Apply

While few congregations today may attempt to crown their preacher as Zeus and offer a sacrifice to their ministers as gods, we can easily erect personality cults which place the preacher upon a pinnacle of authority and infallibility. Christians should respect their leaders. That respect, however, slips into illicit hero worship when it overlooks moral failure or blurs the lines on godly living. We must not confuse the bringer of the message, who is not worthy of our worship, with the subject of the message, who is.

❓ *Is your particular church culture in any danger of worshipping a messenger? How?*

❓ *What is the opposite danger to church-leader hero-worship?*

Through many hardships

Paul has struggled to convince the crowd he is not a god. No, others convince the crowd to put him to death...

Read Acts 14:19-20

Luke compresses the history in order to keep the narrative moving. He leaves out certain details that he, and ultimately the Holy Spirit, deemed unimportant. Verse 20 leaves out details and raises some questions. Luke indicates a group of disciples, no doubt new believers who came to Christ through Paul's ministry—with Paul, and that Paul survived the stoning and re-entered the city. The next day Paul, his body bruised and broken, and Barnabas depart for Derbe.

The way to the kingdom
Read Acts 14:21-28

Paul and Barnabas backtrack to the places they have already been.

❓ *What is their purpose?*
❓ *What is their message?*

As we have seen, being a follower of Jesus was not theoretical for Paul. He had come to understand, through horrific experiences, the cost of discipleship. He had begun to see "how much he must suffer for my name", as the Lord had told Ananias in Damascus shortly after the apostle's conversion (9:16).

The default position for the church in most of its history has been tribulation and persecution. The servant is not greater than his master (John 15:20). If Jesus suffered, we must expect the same. Most of us will not suffer a physical beating for proclaiming the

gospel. You may, however, receive a psychological stoning as the culture rejects you and dismisses your religious convictions as an antiquated system of beliefs which clings to a bygone age long surpassed by the "glory" of modernity. Paul says, however, that it is through those trials that we will enter the kingdom of heaven. In 2 Corinthians 4, Paul encourages the church by saying that such light, momentary affliction is preparing for us an eternal weight of glory beyond all comparison. Suffering will come. We must endure; for, on the other side of tribulation, is the sweet embrace of our Saviour.

❓ *What do you think the mood was when the team reported back to the church in Antioch (Acts 14:27)?*

☑ Apply

Your testimony can produce the same fruit. When you endure suffering and tribulation, you have no idea how God will use your story to encourage others. The testimony of God's suffering saints nourishes the faith of all God's people.

⌃ Pray

Pray that you would suffer for the gospel with joy. Pray that you would speak of your suffering to other believers with joy. Pray that you would be a faithful witness and a great encourager. And thank God for those who have been, or are, these things for you.

The gospel at stake

Acts 15 records the first church council in church history. Several councils stand as monoliths of doctrinal clarification—Nicea (325), Constantinople (381), Ephesus (431).

Like these, the Council of Jerusalem convened over vital matters central to the gospel.

Acts 14 ended with Paul and Barnabas recounting God's glorious work among the Gentiles to the church in Antioch. This celebration, however, met an abrupt halt...

Read Acts 15:1-2

- ❓ *Why (v 1)?*
- ❓ *What did these "certain people" teach that Christians had to do in order to be saved (v 1)?*

Paul and Barnabas stood against this message (v 2). The church at Antioch decided that the matter needed discussing with the church leaders in Jerusalem. So Paul and Barnabas and a wider group were sent to seek their counsel.

Read Acts 15:3-7a

Again, the testimony of the gospel's spread gave cause for celebration (v 3-4). Again, though, this was cut short by the objection from believers "who belonged to the party of the Pharisees" (v 5).

Two points are worth noting here. First, Luke calls these people "believers". Christians will have disagreements, and on important matters. What matters is how we handle conflict. Second, we should praise God for his grace that there were believers from "the party of the Pharisees". The Pharisees had hated Jesus in the Gospels—but

clearly more of them than just Paul himself had repented and believed.

The debate continued until a hush fell as Peter, the rock, one of Jesus' closest disciples, stood to address the crowd (v 7a).

Read Acts 15:7b-11

- ❓ *What does Peter remind the council of (v 7b-8—read 10:9-16, 22-23, 34-48)?*
- ❓ *What had God done for those Gentiles' hearts (15:9)?*
- ❓ *What does Peter accuse the opponents of Paul and Barnabas' of doing (v 10)?*
- ❓ *What does Peter affirm about how both Jews and Gentiles can be saved (v 11)?*

Paul, Barnabas, and now Peter understood the danger to the gospel of the teaching of "the party of the Pharisees". The saving and authentic power of the gospel was at stake.

We'll discover the verdict of the council tomorrow. But for now...

⌃ Pray

Thank God for truth, and for those who are prepared to stand up for it. Ask God for discernment in churches today, to see the difference between unnecessary dispute and arguing for the sake of the gospel. Thank God that he does not discriminate but purifies the hearts of all who turn to him by faith. Pray for unity in the church around the great truth that "it is through the grace of our Lord Jesus that we are saved".

Live saved, live united

Paul and Barnabas have opposed the teaching that obedience to the Law of Moses is necessary to be saved. Peter has supported their position. Now comes the verdict...

James' judgment

Read Acts 15:12-21

This James who spoke up was the brother of the Lord Jesus and the author of the biblical book which bears his name. He had clearly risen to prominence in the Jerusalem church and now served as its primary leader.

❷ *Where does he turn for help (v 15-18)?*

In doing this, James recalls the very voice of God, who spoke through the prophets his plan of redemption, which would rebuild the house of David with a new remnant—a multitude of people from all the nations. When Jesus established the new kingdom, he fulfilled the prophetic promise and restored the house of David, which would include Jews and Gentiles.

❷ *How would this have been helpful in persuading the believing "party of the Pharisees" of the position being promoted by Paul, Barnabas and Simon Peter?*
❷ *What is James' judgment (v 19)?*

In other words, the Gentiles do not need to keep the circumcision laws prescribed in the Old Testament, because their inclusion in the family of God rests on faith in Christ.

❷ *What does James add (v 20-21)?*

James calls on Gentile Christians to not offend Jewish believers through their actions in what they eat and in how they conduct themselves in their relationships.

⌃ Pray

Gospel unity is a precious but fragile thing. Pray that you would always contribute to it, and never undermine it.

Neither Pharisee nor flippant

The outcome of the council's deliberations should call all of us to assess our own understanding of the gospel. Christians can tend towards a Pharisaical view of the gospel, whereby obedience to God eclipses our view of, and our need for, the cross. On the other hand, we can let our rest in the grace of God lead to a flippant life, which disregards the transformative powers of the gospel. In both cases, we need to repent. If we tend towards Pharasaism, we need to know that our salvation does not rest in obedience but in Christ. Obedience and faithfulness flow naturally from one saved by grace. But if we tend towards flippancy, we need to see the cost of our sin. Jesus paid a terrible price that his people ignore or belittle whenever we view salvation as cheap and holiness as optional, and so choose to live like pagans.

⌄ Apply

❷ *Which do you more naturally tend towards? What will you do about it?*

The joy of gospel mission

The Jerusalem Council has given its verdict. And now it remains only to communicate its verdict—truths that will bring great joy and fuel gospel mission.

The letter is written
Read Acts 15:22-29

> ❓ *How does the letter describe the trouble caused by those who opposed Paul and Barnabas (v 24)?*
> ❓ *How would verses 25-26 have underlined Paul's and Barnabas' credibility as gospel teachers?*

Notice the significance of the last sentence of the letter (v 29). The "party of the Pharisees" would have said *You will be saved if you do these things*. The church leaders wrote "You will do well to avoid these things". Obedience in these areas would be a way of loving their Jewish brothers and sisters, but it would *never* be a requirement for remaining as brothers and sisters.

The letter arrives
Read Acts 15:30-35

> ❓ *How do these verses display the positive impacts the letter had on churches with many Gentile members?*

When right theology greets the people of God, the body is strengthened and the faith of believers' is encouraged.

🔼 Pray

Give thanks for your church and for its leaders. Pray that you would experience ever-increasing truth-centred joy.

The team divides
Read Acts 15:36-41

> ❓ *How do the joy and fellowship of the previous verses come to an abrupt halt?*

Back in Acts 13, John Mark had accompanied Paul and Barnabas on their missionary journey. As that mission turned towards Gentile lands, however, Mark deserted the company. Now, two years or so later, Barnabas wants to bring Mark along with them on their second missionary journey. Barnabas again shows the power of Christian love and forgiveness (he was the first disciple, other than Ananias, to accept Paul as a brother in Christ—see 9:27). Paul, however, does not want Mark to join their company, apparently grounding his view in the demanding needs of the mission and his vision for the gospel.

Who was right? Luke does not tell us. The tragedy is not the separation but the manner of it. There will come a time when gospel labourers need to separate—either because of doctrinal or personal issues. Paul and Barnabas could have separated, still disagreeing, but in a cordial, Christ-honouring way. Instead, they parted in bitterness.

🔽 Apply

> ❓ *Is there any other Christian with whom you need to be reconciled, even if you are still in disagreement over a decision?*

 Bible in a year: Isaiah 28-29 • Mark 7:1-13

New friends, new plans

Acts 16 contains some of the book's most iconic moments. We meet one of Paul's closest trainees and see the Spirit-filled message of salvation accepted by Gentiles.

Enter Timothy
Read Acts 16:1-5

> ❷ How is Timothy (the Timothy to whom Paul would later write the letters of 1 and 2 Timothy) described (Acts 16:2)?
> ❷ What does Paul do before letting Timothy join him and his team (v 3)?

This should strike us as strange—in the previous chapter, a council had convened and rejected the teaching that Paul opposed, that Christians must be circumcised to be saved (15:1). Now Paul (even as he delivers the council's decision, 16:4), seems to oppose the council!

Two points need to be made here: first Timothy was a Jew (v 1). So his mother had violated the Old Testament law by failing to have him circumcised. (The question in Antioch and Jerusalem had been about Gentiles and salvation.) So second, Paul understood that if Timothy were not circumcised, his ministry to Jews would be compromised. Timothy's lack of circumcision was a potential stumbling block. It was a problem the gospel did not need, so Paul took Timothy and circumcised him.

Circumcision did not make Timothy any more of a Christian. But he was willing to endure the procedure for the sake of the gospel, to remove an impediment in his ministry to his countrymen. Only faith can secure salvation. At the same time, some works and acts are wise for evangelism.

✔ Apply

That continues to be the case today. We are called to be "all things to all people so that by all possible means [we] might save some" (1 Corinthians 9:22).

> ❷ Why does living this way tend to make life harder?
> ❷ Are there things you could do, or stop doing, that are not required by God, but which would help you better share the gospel with those you live among?

Enter Macedonia
Read Acts 16:6-10

> ❷ How were Paul's plans thwarted (v 6-7)?
> ❷ What did he end up doing, and why (v 9-10)?
> ❷ What lessons are there in this for us today as God's disciples, do you think?

Note that in this passage, Luke's use of pronouns changes from "they" to "we". Clearly, Luke has joined Paul's party.

⌃ Pray

Ask the Spirit to lead you, in whatever way he chooses, to those who are ready to hear the gospel from your lips today.

Waving, not drowning

David's under fire again, but now his troubles are one notch higher on the intensity scale; his woes are on the brink of engulfing him completely...

Watch the signs of change in David as he prays through his situation.

Read Psalm 143

Under strain
Re-read Psalm 143:1-2

❓ *What does David plead for?*
❓ *What does he appeal to (v 1b, 2b)?*

Shattered
Re-read Psalm 143:3-4

❓ *What has happened to him (v 3a)?*
❓ *How does he feel (v 3b-4)?*

Dry
Re-read Psalm 143:5-6

❓ *What does he do (v 5)?*
❓ *Does this help (v 6)?*

God's care seems to belong entirely in the past (v 5)—with no experience of his favour at the present time (v 6).

Longing
Re-read Psalm 143:7-8

❓ *Which phrases here show how urgent his prayers are?*
❓ *What does he appeal to (v 8b)?*

Dedicating
Re-read Psalm 143:9-10

❓ *What exactly is David asking God for here?*
❓ *What do you think it means to "hide myself" in God?*

Remembering
Re-read Psalm 143:11-12

❓ *What are his requests?*
❓ *What does he grip onto about God's character?*
❓ *How might this sustain him?*

We're not told the outcome... We're just left with the reminder of God's unfailing love to his people (v 12).

✓ Apply

Dark times come to all of us: trouble, doubt, opposition, struggle... When they do, remember this:

- *You're not the first.*
- *You're not alone.*
- *You're not without help.*

A crisis is also the opportunity to take hold of the faithful God.

❓ *Will you do so?*

God opened her heart

How does someone become a Christian? In the conversion that Luke records next, we are shown how it happens.

Read Acts 16:11-14

The businesswoman

❓ *Where do Paul's team go (v 11-13)?*
❓ *Who do they meet (v 14a)?*

It appears Lydia is unmarried; perhaps even a widow. She also runs a business which sells "purple cloth" (v 14) and is probably a fairly wealthy woman. (The colour purple denoted wealth or even royalty, because purple dye was expensive.)

Lydia is also described as a worshipper of God. She's not a Jew; she's a religious Gentile at the river for prayer because she acknowledges Yahweh as the one, true and living God. But she (like Cornelius back in Acts 10) is not a Christian.

Opened to respond

❓ *What does Paul do (16:14)?*
❓ *What does God do (v 14)?*
❓ *What does this tell us about the process of conversion?*

This episode should encourage Christians to faithfully proclaim the gospel with gladness and boldness. As God gave Paul the privilege of leading Lydia to Christ, so too does God give all his people the joy of joining in on his mission to save the lost. God, in his sovereignty, chose his church to serve as his vessels and ambassadors. Knowing this should make believers more desirous to

speak to non-believers, and more committed to pray that God would open their hearts to Jesus' saving power.

☑ Apply

❓ *What difference does it make to realise that God is the great evangelist, and that he's inviting you to share in his work?*
❓ *Who will you pray for, that you'd have an opportunity to share the gospel with them?*
❓ *Where could you go, in order to give yourself the best opportunities to share the gospel?*

Come and stay

Read Acts 16:15

Verse 15 does not mean that *everyone* in Lydia's home was baptised regardless of whether they had made a profession of faith. Luke does not tell us who they were, nor how old they were. He wants to underline something different...

❓ *What does Lydia do (v 15)?*

Those whose hearts the Lord has opened open their homes to his people. Sacrificial and loving hospitality marks the character of believers in Jesus Christ.

☑ Apply

❓ *How will it mark yours?*

An unlikely church

The mission in Philippi has witnessed the conversion of a businesswoman. Now the focus shifts to a female at the other end of the social spectrum…

The slave girl
Read Acts 16:16-24

> ❷ *Who do Paul and the team meet here (v 16-17)?*
> ❷ *What did Paul command (not invite or request!) the spirit to do (v 18)?*

Unlike the movies, the spirit came out of the woman "at that moment".

> ❷ *How do "her owners" respond, and why (v 19-21)?*

The jailer
Read Acts 16:25-34

> ❷ *What is remarkable about Paul and Silas' response to being thrown into prison and pinned in stocks (v 25)?*

Following the earthquake, the jailer assumed all the prisoners had left, and so he prepared to kill himself (v 27), because the punishment for letting prisoners escape was death. When the jailer discovers no prisoner has escaped, he understands something inexplicable has occurred.

> ❷ *What question does the jailer ask in verse 29? How does Paul and Silas' behavior in verse 25 explain why the earthquake prompted him to ask it?*
> ❷ *What must someone do in order to know they will (not might!) be saved (v 31)?*
> ❷ *In what three ways do the Philippian jailer and his household demonstrate*

their new-found faith (one in v 33, two in v 34)?

⌄ Apply

Paul and Silas show character in the midst of difficulty—a powerful testimony for the jailer. He had seen God in Paul and Silas. He had seen the power of the Lord manifested through them and around him. How often do we find ourselves asked questions about the way of salvation? Perhaps many of us fail to exhibit the joy of the gospel in the midst of trials, as Paul and Silas did that night. Let us be those who live that kind of witness, that we might have the opportunity to witness to Christ with our words.

A church in Philippi
Read Acts 16:35-40

The chapter concludes with the departure of Paul and Silas. They leave behind an unlikely group: a rich businesswoman, an ex-slave girl, and a jailor who have become believers—they leave behind a church.

⌃ Pray

Your church is an unlikely collection of believers, who have faith only because God kindly chose to call each of you to "believe in the Lord Jesus". Thank God for each of them now—especially for those who are least like you.

The world upside down

Acts 17 contains some of Paul's most powerful sermons as the gospel powerfully saves Jews and Gentiles alike. Read Romans 1:16. Here is the truth of that verse in action!

Some were persuaded

Read Acts 17:1-4

Thessalonica was a very "Roman" city, with a thriving economy. When the Jews were expelled from Rome around 16 years before these events, many came to this Greek city.

❓ *What did Paul do in the synagogue? Why would this approach to proclaiming the gospel have been effective in this particular setting?*

The idea that the crucified Jesus could be the Jewish Messiah was offensive—but Paul did not shrink from proclaiming it.

❓ *With what result (v 4)?*

Others were jealous

Read Acts 17:5-9

❓ *Why does a riot begin?*

Thessalonica boasted 200,000 residents. This was no small city. The chaos could rapidly escalate out of control and engulf the entire city in violence.

❓ *What do the mob accuse a group of these new Christians of (v 6-7)?*

Christians *should* turn the world upside down (verse 6, ESV). Christians love their fellow believers and serve them so that the cause of the gospel might expand. Christians must proclaim not just another king, but the King of kings and Lord of lords. That is exactly what Christians do when

they faithfully proclaim the gospel. Make no mistake, gospel preaching will turn the world upside down—and that is glorious.

To all three accusations, I hope every Christian would say, "Guilty as charged!"

✓ Apply

❓ *Would you be found guilty on all three charges? Why/why not?*

No neutrality

Notice the three-fold pattern. First, Paul preaches; second, the gospel advances; third, the message elicits an angry response. While some turn from their sins and believe Christ, others oppose it. Whenever the gospel spreads, it will provoke a response. A person cannot answer with neutrality when presented with the message of Christ. Either non-believers will repent or they will turn away. Often, the rejection can turn hostile, which happens here in Acts 17. When the gospel collides with unbelief, it will spark flames of discord and controversy.

⌃ Pray

Thank God that the gospel is powerful to save anyone—including you, and those who live and work around you. Pray that you would be faithful in sharing the gospel and not allow negative responses to stop you— and that you would see the gospel advance in your neighbourhood and/or workplace.

Be like Bereans

After the imprisonment in Philippi and the riot in Thessalonica, Paul and Silas are sent away to Berea, not far inland from Thessalonica.

More noble character

Read Acts 17:10-12

❷ *What is remarkable about what Paul and Silas do when they reach this city (v 10-11)?*

❷ *How do the Bereans respond (v 11)? What is good about this?*

❷ *What is the result (v 12)?*

Preachers must rightly handle the word of truth (2 Timothy 2:15). That is their solemn responsibility. A congregation, however, must test the words of the preacher and ensure that the message accords with God's revelation. The Bereans heard Paul's message, searched the Scriptures, and, by God's grace, came to see the truth of the gospel Paul proclaimed. They then changed their minds, and repented and believed. They came to a saving faith because they heard the gospel and, with humble hearts, sought to understand its claims.

The Christian faith is not a blind faith. The Bible makes authoritative claims that require deep contemplation. Faith, therefore, must not be seen as "jumping off the cliff". Instead, we come to understand, by God's grace, the truth claims of the Scriptures and place our faith in the well-reasoned, well-articulated, power of the gospel. We are to "reflect on what [the Scriptures are] saying" and then we will find that "the Lord will give [us] insight into all this" (2 Timothy 2:7).

☑ Apply

❷ *How does your conduct compare to that of the Bereans in how you...*
  - *listen to a sermon on a Sunday?*
  - *read God's word during the week?*

❷ *Over the next two months, how could you become increasingly "Berean-like"?*

The same again

In Berea, Paul has preached. The gospel has advanced.

❷ *What should we expect to take place next...?*

Read Acts 17:11-15

❷ *What causes the trouble in Berea?*

❷ *How do you think Paul and his team might have felt when this began?*

So once more, the new Christians send Paul away for his own safety.

❷ *Where does he now find himself, all on his own (v 15)?*

▲ Pray

Ask God to help you to become more like Paul in your determination to share the gospel message, and more like the Bereans in your determination to be shaped by that gospel message.

Lethargy or passion?

Paul now finds himself in Athens—the birthplace of democracy and the intellectual centre of the Roman Empire. But he's not particularly impressed by what he sees…

Paul and the city

Read Acts 17:16-18

❓ *What does Paul see, and how does it make him feel (v 16)?*

The people had erected idols with their own hands and bowed down to them as gods. They served carved images rather than the one true God.

❓ *Provoked by what he sees, what does Paul do (v 17)?*

Christians must adopt the same heart and mindset as Paul. Too often, we look at the world around us apathetically—we see people worshipping idols, but outrage does not fill our hearts as we see glory given to another. Indifference replaces zeal and lethargy overruns passion. When God's people see idols worshipped, a righteous anger should burn within our souls. With the blast of a trumpet, the Christian must charge into battle, seeking to storm the gates of the enemy, obliterate the idols, and bring the captives to see the only One worthy of worship.

Paul and the thinkers

❓ *As Paul seeks to share the gospel in the market-place, which other worldviews does he come across (v 18)?*

❓ *What does the response (v 18) suggest Paul emphasised in his evangelism?*

Epicureans believed that the gods had no interest or influence in the affairs of humanity. The gods, therefore, had removed themselves from the world. The Stoics, however, believed in a supreme god, yet within a polytheistic worldview—one god among many gods. The Epicureans tended to see life as a matter of chance, while the Stoics viewed the world through a fatalistic lens.

☑ Apply

❓ *How do we see these two views of life around us today?*

❓ *How does the gospel challenge those views and offer a view of the world that is not just true but better?*

Paul's invitation

Read Acts 17:19-21

The Areopagus was the place where the great temples were sited and where thinkers met. Their curiosity to hear Paul's new teaching was evident (v 20)—and so they were willing to hear his gospel message.

⌃ Pray

Paul witnessed in the religious places, the open places, and the elite places.

❓ *Where has God called you to witness?*

Pray that he would direct your steps today towards places where you will have the chance to proclaim the resurrection.

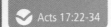
Connect and confront

We now reach perhaps Paul's most famous speech of all—his sermon to the intellectual elite of the city of Athens.

Read Acts 17:22-31

- ❷ *Why do you think Paul began as he did?*
- ❷ *What does Paul say about...*
  - *God?*   *Jesus?*
- ❷ *In what ways does he challenge his listeners?*

The God you don't know

Paul's words at the start of verse 22 might initially appear to be a compliment to the Athenians' religiosity, but in the context Paul meant something different. In verse 23, Paul first depersonalised their worship by not calling the object of their worship "gods" but "objects". Next, he asserted their ignorance of the one true God. Lastly, Paul pointed out that they were "ignorant".

God doesn't need you

In verses 24-26, Paul teaches the doctrines of creation and of God's sovereignty. In doing so, he tells the Athenians that the real God is "not served by human hands, as if he needed anything" (v 25). They needed God for everything (and not the other way around). And God had worked sovereignly so that people "would seek him and perhaps reach out for him and find him" (v 27).

Paul has not yet mentioned Jesus or the Messiah! Instead of quoting from the Scriptures, he is pointing out what the city's own poets recognise. The lines Paul quotes would have likely been written about Zeus, the primary pagan god of Greek mythology. Paul utilises the gems of truth embedded even within their pagan culture. He approaches his audience on their own grounds. He uses what would have been familiar from their own worldview in order to build a bridge that connects the message of the gospel with their pagan mindset.

God calls for repentance

From verse 29 on, Paul challenges his audience: not to think they can make, or imagine, God in their own image (since in truth, they are made in his); but to know that ignorance needs to be repented of, and that judgment is coming and the proof of this lies in the resurrection of Jesus Christ. Paul has contextualised the message, but he will not leave out the gospel or its implications.

The response
Read Acts 17:32-34

- ❷ *What three responses does Paul meet?*

☑ Apply

- ❷ *What does the way Paul presents his message at the Areopagus teach you about the way you can best present that same message to the people God has placed around you? (Hint: think about the dominant worldviews, and how the gospel both connects with and confronts them.)*

Past, present, future

David is looking back to a time when he received help in subduing the enemies he faced. But this is not just nostalgia. He is looking to God for help in the future…

Past: thanks
Read Psalm 144:1-4

> ❓ *What thoughts have set David singing (v 1-2)?*

"Rock" combines (in the Bible) the ideas of strength, changelessness, refuge and provision. What a description of God! Note: he is both a "loving God" and a fortress, stronghold, and so on.

> ❓ *Why is it great that both are true?*
> ❓ *What is the shocking contrast between God and humans (v 3-4)?*
> ❓ *How amazing is it, therefore, that God acts the way he does?*

Present: tense
Read Psalm 144:5-11

> ❓ *What's David's prayer in his new time of trouble (v 5-8)?*
> ❓ *What shows his confidence in God (v 9-11)?*

Future: hope
Read Psalm 144:10-15

> ❓ *What does David look forward to (v 12-14):*
>   • *for his family?*
>   • *for the nation of God's people?*
> ❓ *What does he remain sure of (v 15b)?*

Current: trusting

This psalm has shown us a king, given victory by God, who benefits his people…

> ❓ *Remind you of anyone?*

Of course, this psalm is pointing us to "great David's greater Son", the Lord Jesus Christ. Those who trust in Jesus share in the benefits of his victory and look ahead to a glorious, eternal future.

⌃ Pray

There's plenty to praise God for in this sweet poem. Go on, spend some time now:

• thanking God for how he has blessed you in the past.

• praying for your present struggles.

• praising him for your sure hope of eternal life through Jesus.

Working two jobs

Paul's mission shifts to the city of Corinth, the crossroad of East and West, where he will spend more than a year.

Corinth was a city dedicated to the Greek goddess Aphrodite, the godess of love. Corinth, therefore, knew how to worship. The city worshipped sexual experience. When Paul proclaimed the truth and grace of the gospel, he attacked two foundations in Corinth. First, Paul dismantled the pluralistic worldview of Greek religion. Second, Paul called for the citizens of Corinth to turn away from their sexual immorality and pursue the Lord (1 Corinthians 6:18-20).

Read Acts 18:1-8

> ❓ *What did Paul do in Corinth (v 2-3)?*
> ❓ *What else did he do (v 4)?*
> ❓ *Read 1 Corinthians 2:1-5. What was the heart of Paul's message in Corinth?*

Why labour as a tentmaker? Paul certainly believed preachers of the gospel deserved wages and payment (1 Corinthians 9:14; 1 Timothy 5:18). Taking time to make and repair tents would have meant Paul did not spend every minute he had to preach the gospel and evangelise the lost. Paul tells us in 1 Corinthians: "What then is my reward? That in my preaching I may present the gospel free of charge, so as not to make full use of my right in the gospel" (1 Corinthians 9 v 18). Paul worked in order to make clear that he was not preaching for profit—that gospel proclamation was not a lucrative act but a declaration of grace, offered by grace.

Previously, we have seen this order: Paul preaches → the gospel advances → opposition comes.

> ❓ *How is the order different in Corinth?*

In shaking out his clothes (Acts 18:6), Paul is alluding to Nehemiah 5:13. A robe would most likely have contained dust, leaves, and debris which would fall to the ground in stark symbolism. Paul condemns the Jews who reject the gospel by saying, in effect, that God has shaken them out. Then he refers to Ezekiel 33:1-5—like a watchman, Paul has blown the trumpet of warning in the gospel, and so the blood of those who reject him is on their own hands. Paul will focus his ministry on the Gentiles (Acts 18:6).

☑ Apply

God calls his people to faithfulness, not necessarily fruitfulness. We cannot save another person from their sin. Our job, our calling, our mission is to preach the gospel of Jesus Christ. That is our task and our responsibility. The work of salvation, however, belongs in the sovereign hands of our God. We can preach with confidence, knowing that we cannot fail. We only fail if we remain silent.

> ❓ *Is this your view of evangelism? How should remembering this shape your thinking, your prayers and your actions?*

Keep on speaking

In this remarkable passage, we not only discover why Paul stayed in Corinth for so long but how Paul was sustained in all the suffering that his mission entailed.

Don't be afraid

Read Acts 18:9-11

> ❷ *What commands was Paul given?*
> ❷ *What promise was he given?*
> ❷ *How did he respond (v 11)?*

God had his people in the city, and Paul would see them come to faith in Christ. God, therefore, commands Paul to dispense with his fear. Paul must trust in God's power, his provision, and his sovereign will. Paul heard this word and believed it.

The three imperatives given in verses 9-11 bear significance for all believers. Fear must not mark the children of God. Indeed, as Paul wrote in Romans 8:15, "The Spirit ... does not make you slaves, so that you live in fear." Fear is the very antithesis of faith.

God's people must always speak and proclaim the gospel. Sharing the faith is not contingent upon our circumstances or trials. Our feelings do not dictate when we are to proclaim God's truth. We must go on speaking the good news of the gospel because of the mission to which God has called his people. God says, "Do not be silent". The mission is too grave, the conse-quences too great, the rewards too glorious to remain silent! Eternal souls hang in the balance. We cannot and must not be a silent people, for the message we proclaim is nothing less than eternal redemption.

⌃ Pray

Thank God that he is with you as you serve him. Thank God that he works through his people to reach those who will become his people. Pray that, however long he calls you to live where you do, you would keep on speaking the gospel and never be silenced.

Promise kept

Read Acts 18:12-17

> ❷ *What is Paul charged with (v 13)?*

Under Roman law, an individual could not convert Roman citizens to a foreign cult or religious faction. With this law in mind, the Jews brought Paul to court, hoping to have him condemned and executed.

> ❷ *How well do their plans go (v 14-16)?*

Verse 17 is unclear—who seized Sosthenes, and why did they beat him? I think the most likely option is that it was a Gentile mob, angry with Sosthenes for trying to stir up trouble. What is clear is that the leader of the attempt to persecute Paul ends up suffering himself. And what is also clear is that God is indeed with Paul, ensuring that no one will attack and harm him in Corinth. God keeps his promises.

⌄ Apply

> ❷ *God keeps his promises. How do you need to remember that fact today?*

Giving God our all

This passage reminds us that we should be submitting all that we are, all that we do, and all that we teach to the will of God.

All that we are
Read Acts 18:18

Luke's inclusion of the words "hair" and "vow" lead to the conclusion that Paul had taken the Nazirite vow (read Numbers 6:1-21). But why would Paul, who time and again had preached of God's grace and salvation apart from works of the law, engage in an Old Testament ritual?! Freed by the gospel, he could engage in the ritual with an entirely new perspective. He may have made the vow as an act of devotion to God and an expression of thanksgiving. He also may have entered into the vow in order to appease those Christian leaders who still held their Jewish heritage with high regard. Paul willingly surrendered his rights for the spiritual advancement of others. He devoted his life to enrich the lives of others. We have much to learn from Paul's example. There is no cost which Christian love should count too great. **Read Philippians 2:3.**

All that we do
Read Acts 18:19-23

> ❓ *What does Paul know that dictates his travel schedule (v 20-21)?*
> ❓ *What does he do on his travels (v 23)?*

Paul centred his vision on the will of God. Whether there was success or failure, conversions or condemnations, Paul remained committed to God's will—even if that meant leaving in a time of ministry fruitfulness.

There are times when it is harder to know what God's will is than in others, and there are times when we must simply humbly obey and discover it as we walk in faith. But at all times, we must be seeking God's will in his word, praying for God's leading in our lives, and living to serve his people.

All that we teach
Read Acts 18:24-28

Apollos had been instructed in the way of the Lord (v 25)—he knew of "the baptism of John". This enabled him to speak with fervour (v 25-26) about the things concerning Jesus. But his knowledge was incomplete—he appears to have known only of John's ministry, anticipating the Messiah, and not the ministry of the Messiah himself.

> ❓ *How does this learned Alexandrian show remarkable humility in v 26-27?*

Priscilla and Aquila value the truth more than their own comfort; Apollos more than his reputation. Pride destroys the church—when God's people live humbly, they strengthen the bond of God's people.

⌄ Apply

> ❓ *What will it look like this week to:*
> * *serve God in all you do?*
> * *submit your plans to God's will?*
> * *teach God's truth, and be teachable by God's truth?*

Do you know Jesus?

We now reach one of the most action-packed episodes of all of Paul's church-planting efforts—his ministry in Ephesus.

Deficient faith
Read Acts 19:1-10

- ❓ *What was lacking in the belief of these "disciples" (v 2-4)?*
- ❓ *What outward signs accompanied the inward reality of their faith (v 5-6)?*

Notice the designation of these men as "disciples" (v 1)—but of what or whom? We must exercise caution when dealing with someone who claims to be a believer. Do they actually know Jesus as their Lord and Saviour? Are they actually showing the fruit of the Spirit in their life? Just because someone claims to follow Jesus, does not mean they are saved. Paul lovingly corrects these disciples and boldly points to the deficiencies present in their faith. We ought to demonstrate the same wisdom, grace, and confidence in the gospel message when we have opportunities to correct our confused contemporaries. At the same time, be warned of always trying to "be right". Pride can lead a person to a nitpicky judgementalism that fails to exude compassion and gentleness when dealing with others.

- ❓ *How do verses 8-10 describe the usual course of Paul's ministry in a city?*

Jesus won't be used
Read Acts 19:11-16

- ❓ *What does God do through Paul (v 11-12)?*

- ❓ *What does this prompt Sceva's sons to do, and with what result (v 13-16)?*

Like the sons of Sceva, many in our own day similarly invoke Jesus without really knowing him. They are ready to invoke a sweet Jesus who will be their constant companion and spiritual talisman, but they are not interested in knowing Jesus as the incarnate Son of God. They want a Jesus they can use, not a Jesus who saves—a Jesus they can summon up when they like, not a Jesus who they follow as Lord.

Burning the books
Read Acts 19:17-22

- ❓ *How do the actions of the Ephesians show what true repentance is?*

✔ Apply

True repentance is both public and costly.

- ❓ *Do you love or worship something more than Jesus? What would repentance mean for you—what would be the equivalent for you of the Ephesian Christians burning their scrolls?*

▲ Pray

Thank God for those who first explained the Christian faith to you.

Pray that you would live with Jesus as your Lord to obey, not a genie to be summoned.

Bible in a year: Isaiah 60-61 • Mark 14:1-26

No room for co-existence

Paul has set his course for Jerusalem and then Rome (v 21). But for now, he is in Ephesus—and "a great disturbance about the Way" is about to be provoked.

Read Acts 19:23 – 20:1

❓ *Why is Demetrius so opposed to "the Way", i.e. Christianity (19:24-27)?*

Artemis' temple was one of the Seven Wonders of the Ancient World, as it was the biggest building in the world at the time. No city was as proud of its glorious structures as Ephesus was of this temple. Demetrius' business capitalised on this.

When the gospel comes into contact with other ways of doing life, it will cause friction. When Christians proclaim the gospel, they will not only meet lost souls but lost institutions that will war with the principles of the biblical ethic. In our world, just as in Paul's day, there will sometimes be no way for the gospel and society to peacefully co-exist, and the backlash from society might be fierce, particularly when the gospel threatens livelihoods.

Don't miss the irony in verse 27. If indeed Artemis reigned as a powerful and magnificent goddess, would she really need the work of a mere silversmith to defend her honour?! But of course, this was never so much about giving Artemis honour as worshipping the god of profit.

❓ *What does Demetrius' speech cause (v 28-34)?*
❓ *How does the city clerk calm the rioters down (v 35-40)?*

At the heart of this riot was the monotheism of the Christian faith (though many in the crowd did not even know this, v 32). Monotheism is the defining theological issue in the context of religious pluralism, now as then. As in Ephesus, the masses will attempt to drown out our message with their own (v 33-34). Christians need not shrink back in fear at this kind of opposition.

Indeed, Christians must discern the difference between those who start the riots and those who merely shout a pagan mantra because that seems to be the popular anthem. We should not let intimidation grip our hearts when we encounter a person very confident in their own position on, for instance, the incompatibility of religion and science, or the authority of the Scriptures. Behind the confident tone may be nothing more than a foundation built on sand. We must have the audacity, based upon the truth of God's word, to say there is only one God, and that he has revealed himself in Jesus Christ, his Son.

✓ Apply

❓ *How have you experienced friction between the gospel and the claims and "gods" of your culture?*
❓ *How has your time following Paul in Acts 13 – 19 given you confidence to continue to live for Christ and speak of Christ in the place God has put you?*

GALATIANS: Freedom!

Few books have more profoundly influenced minds or shaped the course of human history than Paul's letter to the Galatians. Martin Luther even called Galatians his "wife"!

A man under authority

It's tempting to quickly skip these introductory verses, assuming they won't have much to offer. But New Testament letters are often laden with precious treasures in their opening remarks. Let's get digging...

Read Galatians 1:1-2a

> ❷ *What do you notice about the way Paul describes himself, both positively and negatively?*
> ❷ *What might he be wanting to clarify or correct?*

"Apostle" literally meant "sent one" but came to have a technical meaning, describing those individuals who were uniquely commissioned by Jesus to lead and teach—and to write authoritative Scripture under the guidance of the Holy Spirit (see John 14:25-27).

A man with a message

Read Galatians 1:2b-5

The "churches in Galatia" probably refers to the churches Paul helped plant on his first missionary journey (see Acts 13 – 14): namely, Pisidian Antioch, Iconium, Lystra and Derbe. As in Paul's other letters, he begins with a kind of "prayer greeting". Typically these greetings highlight key themes that will occur throughout the letter.

> ❷ *What stands out in this greeting?*

The word "age", meaning a period of time, occurs three times in these verses: once in Galatians 1:4 and twice in verse 5 (literally, "for the ages of the ages, amen").

> ❷ *What contrast is Paul therefore making?*

⌄ Apply

Try putting Paul's summary of the gospel here into your own words. What similarities and differences are there with how you typically explain the gospel?

> ❷ *Given what Paul has said about himself (v 1-2a), what difference should it make to how we treat his message (v 2b-5)?*

I'll finish as I started

Read Galatians 6:11-18

> ❷ *What does Paul seem most passionate about in this closing section?*
> ❷ *Paul often comes back to his key themes in the closing section of his letters. Do you notice any parallels between 1:1-5 and 6:11-18?*

⌃ Pray

Throughout church history, the letter to the Galatians has been a powerful tool that God has used to refocus the church on the gospel of grace. Pray that God might graciously be at work through his word in your life.

Astonished apostle

Right, seatbelt on? Seat in take-off position and lap-tray folded up neatly? I hope so. Because we're in for a quite a take-off…

Only one gospel

Read Galatians 1:6-9

- ❓ *What do you sense is Paul's tone in these verses? Why?*
- ❓ *From what you know of Paul's other letters, how does this opening compare? (Scan through a couple of the following: Romans 1:8-15; 1 Corinthians 1:4-9; Philippians 1:3-11; Colossians 1:3-8.)*
- ❓ *What does this contrast show us?*
- ❓ *What is Paul's analysis of what is happening in the Galatian church?*
- ❓ *How do you feel about Paul's response in Galatians 1:8-9?*

Moving away from the gospel is often a subtle business. Nowhere in Galatians are we given the impression that Paul's opponents were no longer talking about believing in Jesus. Much of their language seemed Christian, and yet "under the bonnet" the gospel had been distorted.

What really matters

Read Galatians 1:10

- ❓ *What clues does verse 10 give us for understanding the accusations Paul may have been facing from those in Galatia?*
- ❓ *How do verses 6-9 back up Paul's claim (v 10) that he's not interested in trying to please people?*

We haven't yet been told exactly how the Galatians were being led astray to a "different gospel", but it seems that Paul may have been portrayed as championing a "soft-touch" gospel, in order to win more people to his ministry. Perhaps his message was being labelled as too straightforward or the required gospel response as being too simple. In response, Paul emphasises that his goal is to *please God alone*. If he was interested in mere popularity, then he'd never have become a servant of Christ, nor would he begin a letter by challenging people about preaching a different gospel (v 8-9).

▼ Apply

- ❓ *Do you think turning to a different gospel would ever be a possibility for you? Why/why not?*
- ❓ *Would the apostle Paul be more worried if we answered the previous question in the negative or the positive?*
- ❓ *How does Paul's tone in these verses challenge your attitude to the gospel?*
- ❓ *How do you think we can safeguard ourselves and each other from moving away from "the grace of Christ"?*

A #nofilter gospel

If Paul is to persuade us that shifting to a different gospel is a clear and present danger, then he needs to persuade us that the gospel he preaches is not simply his own invention…

The real deal

❷ *If you wanted to hatch a plan to undermine Paul's gospel ministry, what steps might you take?*

Many of us are familiar with Paul's Damascus Road conversion, as recounted by Luke (Acts 9:1-19). In today's passage Paul gives us his own retelling, but he has a very specific purpose in mind.

Read Galatians 1:11-12

❷ *What is the big point Paul wants to communicate?*
❷ *How does this follow on from Paul's statement that he doesn't glamourise the gospel for his listeners (v 10)?*

Unfiltered origins

Read Galatians 1:13-17

❷ *How does the way Paul describes his former life in Judaism persuade us that he's not a people-pleaser?*
❷ *What does Paul point out in verses 16-17?*

Paul's language parallels the callings of the great Old Testament prophets, Isaiah and Jeremiah (see Isaiah 49:1; Jeremiah 1:5). This isn't about a lifestyle choice or seeking a platform. He knew God had called him to preach Jesus to the Gentiles (non-Jews)— and ultimately that's why he didn't need anyone's endorsement.

The apostle's diary

Read Galatians 1:18-24

❷ *What does Paul seem to be at pains to emphasise in verses 18-24?*
❷ *How does this follow-on from his point about the origins of his gospel in v 11-12?*
❷ *Re-read verse 1. Is there a connection?*

We might assume that close association with the other apostles would bolster Paul's reputation, but Paul thinks it would suggest he's dependent on them. This isn't about Paul being arrogant—having directly encountered Jesus Christ, he wants us to know he didn't get this message from anyone else!

▾ Apply

I wonder how you feel reading Paul's account of his conversion and apostolic calling. Maybe it seems "out of this world"—or at least outside of your own experience. But in a sense that's the point. As a genuine apostle, his commission came directly from Jesus. He is a unique case.

❷ *How can this give us greater confidence about Paul's ministry and the teaching he has written down for us?*
❷ *Are you ever tempted to think the gospel is merely a human creation?*
❷ *Perhaps we're accused of taking the Christian faith "too seriously". How does seeing the roots of the gospel message here help us?*

Freedom fighters

How would you describe the Christian life? Hard? Full-on? Complicated? Sure, but what about "free"? Maybe it's hardly the first thing that comes to mind!

And yet in Galatians we'll see that preserving the gospel is all about protecting Christian freedom.

Trouble in Jerusalem

Having made it clear that his ministry and message did not originate with the other apostles, Paul now explains why he then chose to visit some of those apostles fourteen years later.

Read Galatians 2:1-5

> ❓ *According to Paul, what was the purpose of his visit to Jerusalem (v 1-2)?*
> ❓ *What happens—or doesn't happen—to Titus, and why might this be significant given Titus' background (v 3-4)?*
> ❓ *What do you notice about the language Paul uses to comment on the incident (v 4-5)? Does this surprise you?*

Circumcision might seem far removed from Christianity in the 21st century, but we're going to discover in Galatians that it was one of the big issues then. Male circumcision had been a required mark of those belonging to the nation of Israel, including non-Jews (Gentiles) brought into Israel. The first Christians, who were Jewish, continued the practice. But now the question had arisen as to whether non-Jews who became Christians (like Titus) should also be circumcised.

Given the nod
Read Galatians 2:6-10

> ❓ *What was the outcome of Paul's meeting with the Jerusalem church leaders (v 6-9)?*
> ❓ *What impact might hearing verses 8-10 have upon a church that was being told Paul's gospel was compromised or second-rate?*

Paul is in a difficult situation. He respects the God-given authority of the other apostles and recognises how they've given their blessing to his work. And yet Paul doesn't want to imply that his message is dependent upon them, as this could erode people's confidence if those in Jerusalem changed their mind about what he was teaching.

⌃ Pray

Give thanks for those who first shared the gospel with you—and thank God for those who shared it with them, as well as for the chain of "gospellers" that must go all the way back to Peter's ministry to the Jews or Paul's to the Gentiles (v 7).

Thank God for those who have had to contend in order to preserve the "truth of the gospel" (v 5).

Pray that God might use you to extend that "gospel chain" as you invite people into the freedom of Christ Jesus (v 4), even in the opportunities that today brings.

You are who you eat with

When you were a kid at school, it was a big deal who you sat with at lunch. "Can I sit on your table?" "No, that's where Peter's sitting." Well, some things never change…

Read Acts 10:9-16

For Jews, eating had been governed by a whole series of food laws that set out what and how God's people should eat. Ultimately this meant Jews wouldn't eat with non-Jews. However, with the coming of Christ everything changed. Jesus taught that all foods were now "clean", because ultimately no law or instruction governing external behaviour could change our hearts (Mark 7:19). This was reinforced to Peter when God gave him the vision in Acts 10. As a result, Jewish Christians were now able to eat with non-Jews—but this wasn't to everyone's liking…

Dinner in Antioch

Using Peter's Aramaic name, Cephas, Paul shows us that while he recognises Peter's authority (Galatians 1:18; 2:9), he's not afraid to challenge him either.

Read Galatians 2:11-13

❓ *What seems to have occurred on the "dinner party" scene in Antioch?*
❓ *How does Paul describe Peter's reasons for acting as he did?*
❓ *Why would Paul see Peter's actions as warranting opposing him "to his face"?*

We're not told why these men "came from James", nor whether they complained about Peter's actions, but Peter felt cowed by their presence. Even Barnabas, Paul's fellow worker among the Gentiles, was affected.

Theology on the table

It's likely this incident occurred just before the Jerusalem Council (Acts 15), when it was formally decided that Gentile converts to Christianity didn't need to be circumcised or keep Jewish food laws. Paul could well be on his way to that gathering as he writes this, and so for him this issue couldn't matter more.

Read Galatians 2:14

❓ *What is Paul's analysis of Peter's actions?*
❓ *What do you make of Paul's response throughout verses 11-14? Are you surprised by his reaction?*
❓ *Do you notice any similarities with verses 3-5?*

In theory, Peter's theology hasn't changed: he believes in God's grace for all through Christ. But Paul's analysis shows us that we can undermine this gospel by our actions.

⌄ Apply

We'll be coming back to this issue throughout Galatians, but it's challenging to think that our actions might sometimes "preach" a different gospel to the one on our lips.

❓ *Think of your church community. Does the way you relate to each other ever risk communicating that we are not "one in Christ", by elevating cultural or societal differences?*

One way or another

Mentally swig some strong coffee because today will stretch your brain—but warm your heart too! Paul shows us why the incident in 2:11-14 was so theologically-loaded.

How are we saved?

Remember, Paul has just revealed that he accused Peter of being a hypocrite, for "not acting in line with the truth of the gospel" (2:14).

Read Galatians 2:15-16

> ❷ *What are the key ideas in verses 15-16?*
> ❷ *What contrast does Paul make in verse 16?*

The verb "to justify" is used eight times in Galatians (three times in verse 16 and once in verse 17) and was a legal term meaning to be "in the right with God". It came from the same word as "righteousness" (v 21) and ultimately referred to being given God's future verdict of "righteous" on the day of judgment.

> ❷ *What does Paul expect Peter to know about how all people are "justified" (note his use of the word "we" in v 15-16)?*

···· TIME OUT ····································

Paul frequently uses the phrase "the works of the law" in Galatians (see also 3:2, 5, 10). Some argue that it *only* refers to elements of the Old Testament law that highlighted Jewish communal identity (e.g. circumcision or food laws), but Paul later links these "works of the law" with doing all that was prescribed by the Old Testament law (e.g. 3:10b and 5:3).

Read Galatians 2:17-18

> ❷ *What is the accusation that Paul is anticipating in verse 17?*
> ❷ *How would such an accusation flow out of Paul's case against Peter?*
> ❷ *How does Paul's response pull the carpet out from the feet of his accusers?*

Think of verse 18 not as a direct answer to the question about Christ promoting sin (v 17), but rather as a reflection on Peter's "law-reconstructing" actions in Antioch.

Everything has changed

These next verses are very dense and will get unpacked over the next few chapters, but essentially they "preview" why everything has changed for Christians.

Read Galatians 2:19-21

> ❷ *What connections does Paul make here between the law, Christ's work, and the Christian?*
> ❷ *What is the big conclusion in verse 21 that Paul is wanting us to arrive at?*

⌃ Pray

Working through the complex argument, it's easy to miss the wonder of verses 20-21. Spend some time praising God for these truths and praying that today they would shape our perspective.

Fools!

No one likes being called a fool—and yet Paul uses it twice with the Galatians in today's passage. So what led the Apostle to think they deserved such scornful rebuke?

Finish as you started

As Paul recounted his confrontation with Peter at Antioch (2:11-14) and then explained why it mattered (v 15-21), he gave us a preview of some of the key issues later in this letter. Now he turns to address his readers' own situation and shows how the situations in Antioch and Galatia are worryingly connected...

Read Galatians 3:1-5

❓ *Given the language used, what do you feel is Paul's tone here? Does it remind you of any verses earlier in the letter? (Hint: Try re-reading 1:1-9!)*

The word "flesh" in 3:3 often has a technical meaning in the New Testament, denoting sinful human nature in opposition to God's Spirit: a part of the "present evil age" (see 1:4). In contrast with this, the coming of Christ signals that God is bringing about a new order: the age to come.

❓ *In 3:2-5, Paul asks the Galatians five questions about their own Christian experience. How should they have answered each of them?*
❓ *What does Paul want the Galatians to conclude as they look at their own past?*

It's a common mistake to make: many people default to thinking that the way you stay a Christian is different to the way you *become* a Christian. In effect their gospel is that you *enter* by faith and are *accepted* by grace, but you *stay* by works. Paul is adamant that the way to stay a Christian is the same as how you became a believer in the first place—by faith in Christ's death on the cross. The Christian life is about believing God's promises, rather than partaking in "works of the law" or by the "means of the flesh" (v 2-5).

⌄ Apply

❓ *Do you think Christians today can fall into a similar trap of believing that the way we continue as Christians is different to how we began?*
❓ *In what ways do Paul's questions challenge you personally on this?*
❓ *How does it feel to know that God simply calls us to fix our eyes on the cross of Christ and believe what we heard?*

⌃ Pray

Spend some time gazing upon Christ crucified in your heart and pray that you would look and see him as you go through life today, living by faith in his finished work.

We are family

Like it or not, we're often judged by others by the families we come from. Whether we belong to the "right kind of family" or the wrong kind is significant in all kinds of ways.

Going back to the start

Even today the Old Testament patriarch Abraham is held in high esteem by Jews worldwide. To descend from his lineage is seen as being a recipient of God's blessing.

So it's not hard to imagine why the question of how Christians related to Abraham became hugely important in the first century. As people came to faith in Christ from non-Jewish backgrounds, were they also partakers in the Abrahamic blessing?

Read Genesis 17:1-14

❓ *What did God promise to Abraham in verses 3-8?*
❓ *What was Abraham expected to do in response to this promise (v 9-14)?*
❓ *How extensive was this response to be (v 11-13)?*

Who's your daddy?

Christians from Jewish backgrounds would probably instinctively have seen their connection to Abraham as being through their bloodline. Those from Gentile backgrounds, on the other hand, perhaps felt more like second cousins twice removed through marriage. Into this context, circumcision would have been seen as a powerful way to get closer to Abraham, to receive the family mark.

Read Galatians 3:6-9

❓ *According to the quotation from Genesis 15:6 (Galatians 3:6), how did Abraham receive God's verdict of righteousness?*
❓ *How does this connect Abraham (v 6) to the Galatians (v 1-5)?*
❓ *What do you notice about how Paul describes the promise God made to Abraham (v 8)?*

As we saw in 2:15-21, the verb "to justify" (3:8) comes from the same Greek word as righteousness (v 6). Paul wants us to see that, just as God credited Abraham with a verdict of "righteous" (in spite of his sin), God also promised long ago to give that same righteousness to people of all nations who have faith in him (v 8).

❓ *How would verse 9 have encouraged those Galatian believers who came from Gentile backgrounds?*
❓ *How would it challenge those Jewish-background Christians advocating circumcision?*

☑ Apply

❓ *How do you feel about being spiritually connected to Abraham in exactly the same way as every Jewish-background believer, whether it be Isaac or Jacob, Rahab or Ruth, or Peter and Paul?*
❓ *How would you explain to someone why the promises of Genesis (as quoted in v 8) can truly be good news for them?*

God is...

What do your non-believing friends and relatives think about the God you serve? This psalm will help us—and perhaps them—see him more clearly.

Write down five things that others might say about God (he doesn't exist, he's out of touch, and so on).

-
-
-
-
-

Now read Psalm 145

Excited...

Re-read Psalm 145:1-7

- ❷ *What specific things is David excited about?*
- ❷ *Which one strikes you the most?*

... about God...

Re-read Psalm 145:8-16

- ❷ *How is God described here?*
- ❷ *In what ways is he involved in the world?*

David spoke from his own experience. Christians nowadays should be able to say that they too have experienced the truths here.

- ❷ *Can you think of examples for yourself of the truths in verses 8, 13b, 14, 16?*

... who is great and near...

Re-read Psalm 145:17-21

- ❷ *What encouragements are there here?*

- ❷ *And what warnings?*

... so we should ...

- ❷ *Now list all the responses to this great God that David says we, and others, should be making (verses 1-8).*
  -
  -
  -
  -
  -
  -

Notice that all those responses have to do with communication—talking to God and to others about how great he is.

... and also...

Now (finally) back to your friends' views.

- ❷ *How would you answer each point they have made?*
- ❷ *Why is it so important that you do (v 20)?*

▲ ... Pray

The first step is to get praying: for your friends and for your own knowledge of God and enthusiasm for him. And pray for opportunities to share how great God is with them...

Blessings and curses

If there were a spiritual DNA test to prove whether we're authentic children of Abraham, then faith in God's "gospel" promise would surely be the key indicator.

And having established that faith has always been the way God has made people righteous, Paul is now going to make three statements that prove why the law could never do that.

Law says "Do"

Read Galatians 3:10-12

- ❓ What's so disastrous about relying on "works of the law", according to Paul's first statement (v 10)?
- ❓ How does the quotation from Deuteronomy 27:26 prove this?
- ❓ What evidence does Paul call up in his second statement (Galatians 3:11)?
- ❓ How does the third statement (v 12) seal the deal and prove the law's uselessness in making someone righteous?
- ❓ How would these verses counter the claim that Christians can simply pick and choose those parts of the law that they want to obey, e.g. circumcision?

Jesus says "Done"

Paul has demonstrated to us that the Old Testament law was primarily about "performance": to receive blessing and avoid the curse, you had to "do everything" it demanded. Essentially it was a "doing" system. And the tragedy is that we *all* rely on law by nature. None of us can do *everything* the law demands. And so we are all cursed.

But Paul has also shown us that God had promised—both in Genesis and in Habakkuk (Galatians 3:11)—that those who had faith would be counted as righteous. The obvious question is how those two things can work together: how can people facing God's curse also be made righteous?

Read Galatians 3:13-14

Paul quotes Deuteronomy 21:23, which described how criminals were publicly hung on a wooden post or tree after they'd been killed. This warned others that breaking these laws was punishable by death. And yet here was no criminal...

- ❓ Given the situation God's Old Testament people were facing in Galatians 3:10-12, why is verse 13 so staggering?
- ❓ What do these verses teach us about Jesus' death?
- ❓ According to verse 14, what is the blessing that Gentiles have received through Christ? Is this what you'd expect Paul to say?
- ❓ How does this link us back to verses 1-6?
- ❓ How would you summarise Paul's teaching about the Old Testament law in today's passage?

🔼 Pray

Spend some time reflecting on how Jesus bore the curse of God's judgment in our place, so that we might be freed from that curse to enjoy the gift of God's Spirit.

Know your history

How well do you know your Old Testament—and does it really matter? Today Paul will persuade us that losing sight of our Bible history could jeopardise our spiritual heath.

Law versus Promise

We rewind all the way back to Genesis as Paul shows us the significance of God making a covenant with Abraham.

Read Galatians 3:15-18

❓ *In verses 17-18, what is Paul seeking to prove about the covenant God made?*
❓ *Why is the timing of when the law was first given relevant?*
❓ *How does the example of a human covenant (v 15) illustrate Paul's point?*
❓ *According to verse 16, who were the recipients of God's promises in Genesis? Does this surprise you?*

So why give the law?

If God's covenant can't be changed and the law was never a means of bringing blessing, why did God give the law in the first place?

Read Galatians 3:19-20

To say the law was "added because of transgressions" (v 19) seems frustratingly vague! Arguing that it restrained Israel's sin would be contrary to Paul's law-can't-bring-life argument. Alternatively, to say it *helped* Israel identify their sin is true—but it's likely that Paul actually means the law led to increased transgression (see also Romans 7:7-10). As evidenced in the Old Testament history books, under the law Israel spiralled downwards, making it crystal clear that they needed a different solution to sin.

❓ *Whose arrival is being described in Galatians 3:19?*
❓ *How would the fact that the law was given through angels and mediated by Moses (v 19-20) help bolster Paul's point that it is secondary to the covenant with Abraham?*

A two-faced God?

Read Galatians 3:21-22

❓ *What accusation is Paul trying to refute in verses 21-22? Is he successful?*

Paul's use of the general term "Scripture" (v 22), rather than "law", helps demonstrate that this is all part of God's plan.

The law's use-by date

Read Galatians 3:23-25

Paul has already alluded to the law serving a purpose for a specific time frame (v 9, 22).

❓ *How are this time frame and purpose described here?*
❓ *In what sense is the law an effective "guardian" (v 24)?*

⌄ Apply

❓ *What spiritual confusion can result from misunderstanding God's purposes in giving the Old Testament Law?*
❓ *How does this Bible history help us place ourselves and know how to live in 2019?*

In Christ alone

How would you describe your relationship with Jesus Christ? Do you talk about trusting Jesus, or receiving from Jesus? Would you say you've asked Jesus into your heart?

Here's Paul's take...

See me, see Jesus

We've seen that it has always been *by faith* that people receive God's blessing, just as Abraham did. And we Christians live in a new era of salvation history, with the Old Testament law's role as a "babysitter" over now that Christ has come. But why does Jesus' arrival make such a difference?

Read Galatians 3:26-29

❓ *Jot down all the different references to Jesus Christ in this passage. What strikes you about the way Paul describes the relationship between Christ and Christian believers?*

Paul refers to being "baptised into Christ" in verse 27. While baptism is a physical act, it is likely that Paul is referring to what it represents: a spiritual death and resurrection to new life with Christ. And whether you believe this practice is just for individual believers or includes children of Christian households, the point is that for everyone who is baptised into Christ, their identity is now "Christ".

❓ *What do you think the language of baptism and "being clothed" (v 27) adds to Paul's overall point here?*

❓ *What does Paul mean in verse 28? Why do you think he has chosen these particular categories?*

❓ *Who are the heirs of the promise to Abraham (v 29)—and how does this build on what Paul has already said in verse 16?*

❓ *How do you think this would have gone down in Galatia, given what some were teaching?*

···· **TIME OUT** ····························

Galatians 3:28 is sometimes quoted to argue that there should be no differences between the sexes, e.g. the same roles and responsibilities in church apply equally to women and men. Others use it to argue that maleness and femaleness have actually been abolished in Christ.

❓ *Do you think these are fair applications from the verse in its context here? Why/why not?*

☑ Apply

❓ *How might the way Paul describes the believer's connection to Jesus shape how we understand and explain what it means to be a Christian?*

❓ *How is that different to the way you tend to describe how you became a Christian?*

❓ *What might it look like for a church community to live out the truths of this passage?*

❓ *How might you "re-write" verse 28 to reflect a specific application to your life and your church?*

Heirs and graces

Belonging to Christ makes us heirs to the promise of Abraham. Paul now changes the camera angle on the same gospel truth and shows us the wonder of adoption.

The time of slavery

If we're heirs of the promise, how does this impact upon how we relate to the Old Testament law? Paul begins with an illustration...

Read Galatians 4:1-2

- ❓ *Practically-speaking, why is an underage heir "no different" to the family servant?*
- ❓ *How does this pick up on Paul's description of the law in 3:24?*
- ❓ *What has to change if the heir is to "come into money"? According to 4:2, who determines this?*

Free to be sons

Paul now shows how this illustration makes sense of the Bible's big storyline...

Read Galatians 4:3-5

"Adoption to sonship" (v 5) was a Roman legal term used to describe an adopted male who was now a legal heir.

- ❓ *In Paul's illustration, we were once like an underage heir. How?*
- ❓ *What changed with the coming of Jesus?*

Paul uses particular phrases to describe Jesus in verse 5 (God's Son ... born of a woman ... born under the law).

- ❓ *How do these descriptions relate to what Jesus" has achieved for us?*

"Elemental spiritual forces of the world"

(v 3) is a strange term that describes how humans are spiritually enslaved through material ("worldly") things, often through the wrong belief that these things can help us find our identity and salvation.

Rightful heirs

Read Galatians 4:6-7

In Paul's culture it was the son who received the family inheritance. As such, in verses 6-7 Paul is not being sexist but simply using legal terminology to show that both male and female Christians are adopted as "sons" who inherit God's blessings (see also 3:26).

- ❓ *According to 4:6, what does having the Holy Spirit prove?*
- ❓ *Given verse 7, what would a return to the law show we've misunderstood?*

⌃ Pray

Every family has its faults, but some of us will have particularly sad experiences of family life. Spend some time reflecting on the wonder of being an adopted child of God and having the same relationship with the Father as the Son (v 6).

Give thanks for those you know who have adopted children, and pray for their opportunity to mirror the gospel. You may like to explore this further by reading *Adopted for Life* by Russell Moore, or *Home for Good* by Krish Kandiah.

Stockholm syndrome

Stockholm syndrome is a fascinating and disturbing condition where a hostage develops a fondness for their captor.

Shockingly, we're going to see that Christians can be particularly susceptible to the spiritual equivalent...

Remember where you came from

The wonder of being God's children and heirs of God's promises is all the more staggering precisely because we know this is not something that is our natural state.

Read Galatians 4:8-11

- ❓ *What does verse 8 confirm about the background of those to whom Paul is writing?*
- ❓ *How does Paul also describe our spiritual state before we became Christians?*
- ❓ *Why do you think Paul corrects himself in 4:9a? What do you think is the difference between knowing God and being known by God?*

Moving on is going back

Paul has just described the pagan background of these Gentile Christian converts as slavery, and yet now they are "turning back" to that slavery.

- ❓ *But what's so surprising about what this "turning back" involves (v 10)?*

Given everything else we've seen in Galatians, it's highly likely that these special festivals were part of the Old Testament

calendar. Presumably the Galatians felt such behaviour was a mark of spiritual maturity, and yet in their adherence to parts of the Old Testament law, Paul saw their actions as akin to stepping back into their pre-Christian slavery.

- ❓ *Why do you think observing Jewish festivals was attractive to the Galatians?*
- ❓ *Can you empathise with Paul in v 11?*

⌄ Apply

- ❓ *How does it feel to hear your pre-Christian condition—and the condition of every non-Christian—being described as enslaved?*
- ❓ *Does that change how you think about the gospel?*
- ❓ *Following OT law is described here as slavery. How does it feel to hear that?*
- ❓ *Can you imagine yourself finding such rules and regulations attractive, like the Galatians?*

⌃ Pray

Throughout the Bible, the language of God's knowledge is bound up with him setting his love upon those he personally chooses. And just as he chose Abraham and chose Israel, so he knows and chooses those who trust in Christ. Rejoice that you don't just know God but are known *by* him, and pray that you'd not turn away from him to any form of spiritual slavery.

Ministry midwife

Reading, hearing and sharing God's word can never be a hobby or a classroom subject. It is about real lives, and it brings profound joys as well as fraught anguishes!

Love at first sight?

Given Paul's blunt rhetoric and tight logic, we could perhaps lose sight of the fact that Paul is writing this letter in the context of a genuine relationship.

Read Galatians 4:12-16

❓ *Given the content of Galatians so far, what do think Paul means by his opening plea in verse 12?*

❓ *How might 3:1-5 and 4:8-11 particularly help us understand it?*

❓ *What do we learn here about the history of Paul's relationship with the Galatians?*

❓ *How does the Galatians' previous treatment of Paul demonstrate their response to the gospel?*

❓ *What does Paul think has changed (v 15-16)?*

It's easy to think of the apostle Paul as a grand theologian and fervent church-planter, and to forget that he was someone who got ill and was dependent on others—just like the rest of us! Not only that, but verse 15 may indicate that he particularly struggled with an eye disease. Thankfully the Galatians showed real spiritual understanding and did not reject Paul's weakness but grasped that God uses such means to showcase the power and wisdom of the divine message (see also 1 Corinthians 1:18 – 2:5; 2 Corinthians 12:1-10).

Labour-ward love

Having reminded the Galatians of what their relationship with him used to look like, Paul now shines the spotlight on those who have disrupted this relationship and led the Galatians spiritually astray. Paul has already referenced this group of troublemakers (Galatians 1:7-9; 3:1), and now he begins to bring them into sharper focus.

Read Galatians 4:17-20

❓ *According to Paul, what was the motivation of those who were causing trouble? How did they go about achieving this?*

❓ *What does verse 19 reveal about how Paul understood Christian ministry?*

❓ *How much does this all matter to Paul?*

⌄ Apply

❓ *Would this passage help persuade you to listen to Paul and his message?*

❓ *What would the difference be between a church that generates law-keepers and a church where God forms a Christ-like community?*

❓ *How could our response to those who minister the gospel to us be more like that of the Galatians (e.g. v 14)?*

❓ *How could our attitude to those we are ministering the gospel to be more like that of the apostle Paul (e.g. v 19)?*

Personal praise

The last five songs in the psalter—known as the "Hallelujah Psalms"—are entirely devoted to praising God.

There's no asking for help and no confession, depression or confusion. And surely this is where we should all end up. Following Jesus Christ and living to the glory of God is often confusing, difficult and draining, but in the end, it is our duty and our joy to praise our Maker and Saviour, and to trust him for the parts where life is a struggle.

Read Psalm 146

Who needs help?

- ❓ *Who is the psalmist talking to in verse 1?*
- ❓ *What is he urging himself to do?*
- ❓ *Why do you think he needs to talk to himself like this?*

Other psalms in this last section urge us to encourage *each other* to praise God. Here, the writer is talking to himself. Our hearts, we know, are desperately wicked. And our temptation is to always give in to self-pity when our lives are hard. So we need to keep preaching to ourselves, urging our cold hearts to give God due credit for all that is ours in Christ. The first sign of madness in the Christian life is when we *stop* talking to ourselves!

- ❓ *What sermon do you need to preach to yourself today?*

Who not to praise

- ❓ *Find three reasons in verses 3-4 why it's just plain stupid to praise mere humans.*
- ❓ *How is God the exact opposite of all this?*
- ❓ *How do we thank people properly for things they have done for us or in church, for example, and yet give the glory where it belongs—to God?*

Who to praise

Notice that it's not just *any* Creator God that we need to praise. The God of the Bible is the God who made everything (v 6) but who also cares passionately about people (v 7-9) and about justice (v 7a, 9c). Praising "the unknown God" is just not good enough. Our intelligent worship must be given to the LORD, who reveals himself in Jesus Christ.

⌃ Pray

Read verses 5-10 again, and think how the Lord Jesus fulfils each point through his life, death and resurrection.

Now preach these truths to yourself (v 1), and give voice to your praise. Saying words of praise to God is just the start. A life that praises God truly is a life that becomes like him in how it feels, what it does and what it wants for others...

Sitting comfortably?

Do you know that phrase, "He pulled the rug from under my feet"? That's exactly what Paul's going to try today...

Listen to the law!
Read Galatians 4:21-23

The term "law" was used to refer both to the first five books of the Old Testament and to the specific commands given to Moses at Mount Sinai. Paul is going to use the former, particularly the account of Abraham's sons in Genesis 16 – 17, to highlight that we can't go back to the latter...

❷ *How does Galatians 4:21 clarify Paul's analysis of the Galatians' actions?*
❷ *What difference does Paul highlight between Abraham's two sons (Isaac and Ishmael) in verse 22?*

You may find it helpful to make two columns on paper and write down the various contrasts as we go through the passage.

A tale of two families
Read Galatians 4:24-27

Paul will now "figuratively" (NIV) or "allegorically" (ESV) show how the Old Testament illuminates the situation in Galatia, and we're in for a shock...

❷ *What does Paul say the two mothers represent (v 24)?*
❷ *Which places does Paul associate them with (v 24-26)?*

Add these details to your columns. God's covenant "from Mount Sinai" (v 24) was made with Israel in Exodus 19 – 24.

Although God had redeemed Israel from Egypt (Exodus 19:3-4; 20:2), the covenant clearly required Israel's obedience to the law (Exodus 19:5, 7-8; 24:3-8), hence Paul equating it both with slavery (Galatians 4:1-7) and bringing a curse (3:10-14).

Paul has already implied that many of those insisting on observation of the law were based in Jerusalem (1:18-19; 2:1-6, 11-14), and so Paul contrasts them with the Jerusalem "above" (4:26): the reality of the new creation (6:15). Just as Sarah, Abraham's wife, was childless (Genesis 17:15-22), so God's promises seemed "barren", when Israel ended up in exile and then failed to regain their previous status. And yet Paul cites Isaiah 54:1 to show God had promised to create a fruitful people as part of this promised new creation.

Know your family!
Read Galatians 4:28 – 5:1

❷ *According to Paul, which family do the Galatians—and therefore all Christians—belong to (4:28)?*
❷ *How might they have responded to this?*
❷ *Who does Paul have in view in verses 29-30? What might have been their response?*
❷ *What do you make of 5:1 as a conclusion? How does it expose the foolishness of the Galatians' actions?*

Two ways to live

Although "falling from grace" is often associated with a moral fall, Paul is going to show us that the real danger lies in when we try climbing up to God by ourselves.

Falling from grace

Having urged the Galatians to stand firm in the freedom Christ has given them (5:1), Paul now spells out exactly why he believes the Galatians are throwing this freedom away.

Read Galatians 5:2-6

- ❓ *What do you sense is Paul's tone as you read verse 2?*
- ❓ *Why would being circumcised (v 2-4) be so spiritually dangerous?*
- ❓ *How does this back up 3:10-13?*
- ❓ *How is the Christian life described in 5:5? How does this life compare with the Galatians' version in verses 2-4?*

We saw in chapter 2 that the language of justification and righteousness describe God's future verdict of "righteous" on the day of judgment for those who have faith in Christ. That future verdict is absolutely certain and that fact therefore gives us assurance in the presence, but God's verdict is still something that we "await".

- ❓ *At first glance, verses 3 and 6 seem to be in direct contradiction. Given that circumcision can be spiritually deadly, what does verse 6 mean?*
- ❓ *According to verse 6, what is the evidence that someone is a Christian?*

Abandoning the race

Try reading this imagining that you're a Galatian Christian who has assumed that those advocating circumcision are highly respectable, spiritual Christians.

Read Galatians 5:7-12

- ❓ *List the different ways that Paul describes those causing trouble in Galatia. How do you feel about them?*
- ❓ *How might the Galatians have felt on reading this?*

Apparently some people were accusing Paul of being inconsistent on the practice of circumcision (v 11), probably because he permitted it for missional reasons (see Acts 16:3).

- ❓ *Why do you think Paul equates preaching circumcision with abolishing the "offence of the cross" (Galatians 5:11)?*
- ❓ *How does this connect with 2:12 – 3:1?*
- ❓ *What do you make of Paul's biting humour in 5:12? How does it relate to what's happening in Galatia (v 2-3)?*

✓ Apply

You can't trust in Christ and also trust in something else for spiritual life. It's either/or, not both/and. To turn to circumcision—and therefore the law—meant to turn away from Christ, which meant to fall "away from grace" (v 4).

- ❓ *How does this passage help us recognise the difference between us believing we're justified by Christ and looking to be justified by something else?*

Freedom is...

Undoubtedly freedom has become one of the dominant themes of our age—but what is true freedom? How would you, and people you know, finish the sentence?

Freedom misunderstood

Paul has been crystal clear: "It is for freedom that Christ has set us free" (5:1), so we need to resist distortions of Christianity that imply our relationship with God is based on our own efforts. But that leaves us with an obvious question: *so, how then should we live?*

Read Galatians 5:13

As most Bible footnotes indicate, "flesh" here refers to "the sinful state of human beings"; it's part of the "present evil age" (1:4) and opposed to the work of God's Spirit (3:3).

❷ *Having repeatedly warned us that Christians should not turn back to the Old Testament law, what concern does Paul express in 5:13?*

Verse 13 could also be translated as "Become slaves of one another through love".

❷ *What strikes you about this language of service/slavery, given verses 1 and 13a?*
❷ *Given everything we've seen that Christians receive from God in the gospel, why would love be a fitting response?*

Love rules

Maybe the call to love seems a bit of an anticlimax! Didn't we know that already? But over the next 20 verses Paul wants to blow our minds with a remarkable vision of love—and these next verses are the dynamite.

Read Galatians 5:14-15

❷ *How does verse 14 relate to the previous verse?*
❷ *Given that Paul has been passionately persuading us that we're no longer under the Old Testament law, do you think he's contradicting himself in verse 14?*
❷ *Why/why not?*
❷ *Of all the commands and verses he could have chosen, why do you think Paul chooses to quote Leviticus 19:18 in particular?*

The language of biting and devouring (Galatians 5:15) evokes snake-like imagery, a creature often biblically associated with working against God's purposes.

❷ *How do you think Paul wants us to feel about the prospect of verse 15?*
❷ *How would you summarise the concept of Christian freedom, as Paul describes it here?*

☑ Apply

❷ *How highly do you value love?*
❷ *How do you feel about considering yourself a slave of others?*

We can't be exactly sure of what was happening in Galatia, but perhaps the te~~~tion to embrace the Old Test~~~ was in a part a reaction to~~~ siveness among some Chri.~~~ relevance might this have fo~~~

Holy Fight Club

Keeping religious rules and letting our sinful desires run riot seem like two very different ways to live. And yet Galatians shows that both are forms of the same thing...

... and both are equally deadly. That's because in both we're operating "by means of the flesh" (compare 3:1-6 with 5:13), with the human will set against God. By contrast, today we're going to see what it means to "live by the Spirit".

The battlefield
Read Galatians 5:16-18

The word translated as "live" in the NIV (v 16) is perhaps better translated as "walk" (ESV), giving a sense of daily intentionality and practice.

- ❓ *What assumption does Paul seem to make about Christians who are "walking by the Spirit" in verse 16?*
- ❓ *According to verse 17, what will the Christian life feel like?*
- ❓ *How does verse 18 remind us of the era in which we live? (See also 3:23 and 4:2-6.)*

Sin unleashed
Read Galatians 5:19-21

- ❓ *What do you notice about how Paul introduces the list of "acts of the flesh" in verse 19? Do you find this challenging?*
- ❓ *How do you feel reading through the list? Do you notice any structure to the fifteen behaviours and attitudes listed?*
- ❓ *God often gives warnings as a means of grace to keep his people responding the right way to him. How does v 21 do this?*

Getting fruity
Read Galatians 5:22-24

- ❓ *How do you think Paul wants us to feel as we read through this list?*
- ❓ *Why do you think Paul says, "Against such things there is no law" (v 23)?*
- ❓ *When do you think the event in verse 24 happened? How might the language of crucifixion help us here? (Clue: have a look back at 3:1; 2:20; 1:3-4.)*

⌄ Apply

Sometimes Christians can get discouraged because fighting sin can be such a battle.

- ❓ *What encouragement can you take when you personally feel the fight of 5:17?*
- ❓ *How does verse 24 give you a bigger view of what happened at the cross?*
- ❓ *How will this motivate you to walk by the Spirit today, even if some acts of the flesh may feel natural?*

⌃ Pray

Spend some time reading through the "acts of the flesh" and asking God to convict you in areas where you're tempted to "gratify" these desires. Pray for his help to not use your freedom as an excuse.

Then pray through the "fruit of the Spirit", asking God to captivate you with the beauty of what the Spirit is working to establish.

The Spirit-led life

Having been exhorted to "walk by the Spirit", we now zoom into the nitty-gritty of life, as Paul issues his "step-by-step" guidance for keeping pace with the Spirit.

Step by step

Read Galatians 5:25 – 6:5

❓ *Many Bible translations put a break between 5:26 and 6:1. What might we gain from seeing Paul as being in mid-flow in these verses?*

❓ *How does Paul's pastoral awareness in 6:1 help us as we look out for each other and ourselves?*

❓ *What do you notice about Paul's use of the language of "law" in verse 2? How does this build on 5:13-14?*

❓ *How does 6:2-5 balance communal responsibility and personal accountability? In what ways does this challenge you?*

The common good

Read Galatians 6:6-10

❓ *What similarities do you notice with what Paul said in 5:16-25?*

❓ *How does 6:7-8 develop Paul's warning against license in 5:13?*

Paul mentions supporting our pastor-teachers leaders in 6:6, and seems to develop this into a wider principle about generosity in verses 7-8.

❓ *Does it surprise you that you should consider your finances as part of the Spirit-led life?*

❓ *What do you make of the principle and priority that Paul sets out in verse 10?*

☑ Apply

No one likes admitting to pride (v 3)—and especially not when it's in excess, as in "conceit" (5:26). And yet such unacknowledged self-centredness can be deadly for our spiritual health, both individually and as churches. Perhaps part of the problem is that we see those two areas as very separate and tend towards shutting ourselves off from others. (Compare again 6:2 with v 3!)

❓ *Do you allow others to speak into your life and highlight pride? In what ways might you have isolated yourself and created a blind-spot where conceit can develop?*

❓ *How does the priority that Paul sets in verse 10 help you consider how to use your time, gifts and energy to sow "to please the Spirit" by doing good?*

❓ *Paul keeps reminding us that our "walking" demonstrates whether or not we belong to God's eternal future. How does this challenge you?*

⌃ Pray

Consider your own church family. Give thanks for the different ways you see this Spirit-led community in action.

Pray against the weariness described in verse 9.

Seeing the big picture

As we draw to the end of Galatians, Paul leaves us in no doubt about where our spiritual confidence should lie, and why…

Ashamed of the cross
Read Galatians 6:11-13

Paul's opening comment (v 11) probably indicates that he is now choosing to write this closing section himself, rather than dictating to a scribe.

> ❷ *Why might Paul want to highlight this?*
> ❷ *How does Paul summarise what's happening in Galatia?*

Paul has used the word "compel" (v 12) twice before in the letter, describing what happened both in Jerusalem (2:3-4) and Antioch (2:14, often translated "force").

> ❷ *How do these references help us sense the seriousness of the situation in 6:12?*
> ❷ *What outrageous irony does Paul reveal in verse 13?*
> ❷ *How would all this have left the Galatians feeling?*

Created by the cross
Read Galatians 6:14-18

> ❷ *What contrast does Paul make between his motives (v 14) and those of the troublemakers in Galatia (v 12-13)?*
> ❷ *Why is this situation ultimately about the cross of Christ (v 12, 14)?*
> ❷ *And how is the issue of persecution connected (v 12; see also 5:11)?*

It's not unusual for Paul to end with a prayer for God's peace, but in Galatians there's a unique twist: Paul's prayer has a condition (6:16). Interestingly, the verb he uses ("follow") is also used in 5:25 ("keep in step with"), suggesting a parallel structure. In other words, living by the Spirit is what it means to live as part of the new creation.

> ❷ *How might addressing the Galatians as the "Israel of God" (6:16) be a powerful and fitting way to close this letter?*

✓ Apply

> ❷ *What would it look like for you to echo Paul's prayer in verse 14 for yourself?*

Compare again verses 14-16 and 1:3-5. Christians live as part of the new creation, having been rescued from the "present evil age" through Jesus' death. To boast in that cross is to know that Christ has borne the curse of the law upon himself (3:13), meaning that in his death we too have died, and we now live as new people, redeemed to live by the Spirit. This is a new era; the new creation has dawned.

︿ Pray

Spend some time reflecting on how God has been at work in your heart through Galatians. You may find it helpful to read through the book again and write a series of prayers to reinforce the powerful challenges it contains for our own walk with God, and how we take part in and shape church life.

Enjoying God

Praising God is more than simply singing hymns loudly and with passion. One way we can think of it is that we are advertising God's character and benefits to others.

In the last psalm, we were talking to ourselves. In this one, we hear God's people talking to one another about their great King, Creator and Provider: *Isn't he great!*

Good, pleasant, fitting

Read Psalm 147:1

❓ *What reasons are we given in verse 1 to praise God?*

Sometimes we need to stir ourselves to praise him—by reminding ourselves of what he has done for us. But notice that singing praises should be something that we delight in and enjoy! Our praises should bring us pleasure.

The God who cares

Read Psalm 147:2-6

❓ *What is God doing to and for his people (v 2-6)? Why is it important to remember that as we gather to worship?*

As we sing to each other, we should also remind ourselves of who we really are and the reason we have been brought together:

Gathered exiles—deservedly banished from the garden, and underservingly, but miraculously, brought back into it.

Wounded and broken—but by his mercy and grace, our hearts have been restored and our wounds bound up. As you sit in church next time, look around, and as you see those whom God has been specially gracious to, pause to give thanks for them—and praise to their God and yours.

Being built up—God is doing a work in the world: building his chosen ones into people who bring him glory.

❓ *Which of these verses means most to you...? Why?*

The God who provides

Read Psalm 147:7-11

❓ *What does God love to do (v 8-9)?*

There is the special grace that God works for his people through the gospel, but God's mercy extends to all mankind in the reliability of the seasons, his provision of food for the world, and the wealth of riches he has given us in human love, in art and in nature. We may be impressed by the rippling muscles of men and animals (v 10)...

❓ *... but what does God truly value (v 11)?*

The God who speaks

Read Psalm 147:12-20

The elements are God's to command by his word for blessing to all mankind, but also for the judgment of his enemies and the reproof of his people (v 15-18).

Think about the reality of verses 13, 14, 19 and 20 for you, and then obey verse 12!

COLOSSIANS: The hope

Peace. Provision. Forgiveness. These are basic human needs. Yet who could truly be relied upon to deliver them?

When Paul sat down to write to the Christians in the bustling town of Colossae, the Roman empire claimed that it could deliver these things to its citizens. Paul knows that only God can give these things, and writes this small but powerful letter to make the issues clear for the believers there.

Hello

Read Colossians 1:1-2

❓ *How does Paul describe himself?*
❓ *How does he describe the Colossians?*
❓ *What ideas that are central to the gospel message does he include in his greeting?*

Grace and peace are not hollow platitudes; they are key to what sets Christ's cosmic rule apart from the rule of any human emperor or system. For who else can offer to every person on earth the wonders of God's undeserved forgiveness and mercy? Who else can restore us (and the entire creation) to everything we were created to be? This is real peace.

The gospel

Read Colossians 1:3-8

❓ *How did the Colossians become Christians?*
❓ *How does Paul describe the traits of the Christians in Colossae? Pick out the powerful phrases from these verses.*
❓ *How does he describe the gospel?*

❓ *What is curious about the order of faith ... love ... hope in verses 4-5?*

The logic of how Paul orders the so-called "Christian's trinity" of faith, love and hope is surprising. We might expect to find that love for others and hope of heaven derive from trusting Christ. But here, the lynchpin for faith and love is in fact hope. A Christian's confidence gives them what they need to grow (v 7-8). God's promises in Christ are what makes the Gospel news good: that is, because they are all about that grace we have been given in Christ. The Colossian Christians understood it (v 6) and knew it to be true. That is why they had a sure hope.

☑ Apply

This paragraph raises the obvious question of how someone might report on our own Christian walk.

❓ *What evidence is there that we are "saints" (v 2, ESV) or holy people?*
❓ *Think about your own conversion to Christ. How do you usually describe it? How might you describe it in the way that Paul does in verses 6-8?*
❓ *Genuine faith is never just believing things are true—that is, mere intellectual assent. What else is required to make it real?*

How to grow in faith

If you want to discover a person's real priorities, ask two questions: what do you spend most money on, and what do you most often pray for yourself and others?

A new commitment
Read Colossians 1:9-10

❷ *What does Paul pray for in verse 9?*
❷ *Notice that he prays for this continuously. Why is this so important?*
❷ *What else does he pray for (v 10-12)?*
❷ *How is this different from the kinds of things we often pray for ourselves, in church or in prayer groups?*

Ministry can never be simply about converts completing response cards at an event—it is about making and supporting lifelong disciples. The need to be filled with the knowledge of God's will is constant, and it is the most important thing—because it is from this knowledge of God that genuine God-honouring living springs, so that we might live fruitful lives. Memorising swathes of theology serves little purpose if it stays as head knowledge. The grandest purpose of theological knowledge must be to pursue godly wisdom.

☑ Apply

❷ *If somebody had access to your bank statements and prayer lists, what would they conclude? Who or what is the focus of your life from this evidence?*
❷ *How might you change what you pray for in light of Paul's prayer here?*

God's power
Read Colossians 1:11-14

❷ *What else does Paul pray for?*
❷ *What does this prayer suggest about the Colossians' circumstances?*
❷ *How do the statements in verses 13-14 form the basis of Christian growth?*

Paul wants every Christian to endure to the end. It means keeping going in faith, love and hope until the thing we hope for has been attained. But that is an intimidating thought—especially if the battle with temptation or opposition rages fiercely. The good news is that we are never abandoned to fight this battle alone. Just as the Spirit fills us with wisdom and understanding, so he enables the very perseverance he calls us to. In fact, the most powerful evidence for his invisible work must surely be the fact that believers *still believe* despite their horrendous circumstances. And that they are able to walk through their circumstances with a joy and a thankfulness that is supernatural.

And central to all of this is understanding what God has done for us in the gospel, and how we are now completely different. We may live in Rome, Britain, Australia or America, but we have a different and more permanent address: the kingdom of his beloved Son, Jesus.

❷ *What will you pray now for yourself, and for others?*

Image of God

This letter is scandalous. Its categorical statements about Jesus' uniqueness put Christians on a collision course with Rome back then, and with our modern world now.

Everything!

Read Colossians 1:15-20

❷ *Pick out the universal statements here about Jesus. How many times is the word "all" or "everything" used?*

❷ *What is Jesus not Lord over, according to these verses?*

❷ *What did he achieve when he died on the cross (v 20)?*

Jews would never have struggled to believe that there is only one God and that he created everything that exists. But for the many in Colossae from a pagan background, the idea would have been palpably absurd. They followed many gods and had many myths about the world's origins. But the idea that this unique Creator actually spent time on earth would have baffled both groups. Yet that is precisely what Paul insists had happened just a few years before. The man Jesus is Lord of *everything*. And the picture Paul builds for us is staggering in its scope. He is:

Father: If you want to know what God is like, you need to look at his Son—because he is God's true image. Or, in the words of Hebrews, he is "the exact representation of his [God's] being" (Hebrews 1:3). Like a great portrait, Jesus offers a true likeness of the Father. When we look at Jesus, we see God.

Creator: Paul writes, "For in him all things were created," (Colossians 1:16). It is a staggering claim. If a great artist paints a masterpiece, he or she has full ownership rights over it, right up until the moment it is sold to a collector or given to a friend. Well, Jesus has never done that with his masterpiece. He never would. He made everything. So he owns everything.

Sustainer: Gravity may well exert the most extraordinary forces on everything from insects to planets, yet Jesus Christ, fully God and fully man, is the one on whom it depends second by second. As Paul says, "In him all things hold together" (v 17).

In view of this condensed catalogue of Jesus' qualities, it is no wonder that he has all the rights due to the "firstborn over all creation" (v 15).

⌄ Apply

❷ *Why would people find the statements in this passage so outrageous? What might you say in response to someone who thought these claims ridiculous?*

❷ *Jesus is the image of the invisible God: how would you explain to someone what Christians believe about Jesus and his divinity?*

❷ *Jesus is the sustainer: how should this knowledge change the way we view both Jesus and the universe we live in?*

Mine!

"There is not a square inch in the whole domain of our human existence over which Christ, who is Sovereign over all, does not cry: 'Mine!'" said Abraham Kuyper.

Yet this truth also raises a problem: if it is all his, why doesn't he do something about everything that has gone so badly wrong?

Rescued...

Read Colossians 1:15-20

❓ *Why was Jesus born?*
❓ *Why did Jesus die?*
❓ *Why did Jesus rise again?*
❓ *Why do we need rescuing? What do the verbs in verse 20 suggest?*

Ever since Genesis 3, there has been a simple root cause of all that is wrong in the world—from the grand scale of empires and nations right down to the personal level of playground bullies and marital conflict. It is sin. This is the human heart-attitude that consistently chooses to go it alone. It is a matter of creatures declaring independence from the Creator. We insist that we don't need God or his ways in our lives. Everything needs to be done our own way. That is treason of a cosmic order. We need reconciling because we are estranged from God. We need Jesus to make peace for us because we are at war with God.

... by his blood

Read Colossians 1:20 again

❓ *How is the truth of this verse under attack today?*

❓ *How does Jesus' death on the cross make peace? What do people still find offensive about that claim?*

The ancient Greek mindset took a highly negative view of all things physical and bodily. For a culture that prized the more "spiritual" realm of ideas and the mind, the body seemed to let the side down. But that is not God's style. He created the body and so is entirely pleased to embrace the reality of having a body. Bodies cannot be so bad after all, it seems. God's purpose in the Son becoming fully human goes far beyond simply proving that, however. He was pleased for this precisely because he was pleased to rescue his creation. And becoming human was fundamental to achieving that.

Result

❓ *What is Jesus' relationship with his people—the church (v 18)?*

The extraordinary thing is that the evidence of God's work of new creation is the existence of the church. God's evidence includes the church that meets down your street; and the fellowship nearby that gets up to some slightly whacky activities that you don't fully understand or accept; plus the tiny group of brothers and sisters forced to meet in secret because of an oppressive government regime. All of these are expressions of God's people living out their faith. As such, all are evidence that God is bringing about a new creation.

Radical conversion

Christians are people with a past, a present and a future. And in order to serve Jesus, live well, and grow to maturity, we need to understand all three of these realities.

Past
Read Colossians 1:21

- **?** *What were we once?*
- **?** *Does this description resonate with your own experience? Why/Why not?*

It's a devastating diagnosis: alienated from God. We were hostile in our minds. Our thinking was opposed to seeing things the way God sees things. And we were doing *evil* deeds. You may have grown up respectable and well-behaved; you may have been part of a Christian family, and never remember a time when Jesus was not real to you; but you know the truth of these verses. On the outside we can look moral and "good", but we know that all our righteousness is like filthy rags.

Present
Read Colossians 1:22

- **?** *What has Jesus done for us?*
- **?** *How did he do it?*
- **?** *For what purpose did he do it?*

Reconciliation is one of the most beautiful concepts in human experience, but it is also complex. It speaks of the joy of friendship but also the pain of relationship breakdown. Reconciliation can only come about if both sides agree to it, and it always requires humility. It requires the readiness to deal with the causes of that breakdown and the desire to rebuild. In short, reconciliation is hard.

And for cosmic rebellion, reconciliation required sacrifice, blood, death—the cross. The curious expression "his body of flesh" (ESV) or "Christ's physical body" (NIV) underlines that this reconciliation demanded both the incarnation and the real suffering and death of Christ to break open a way back to God for the whole of humanity. Our current status is that we are reconciled to God.

Future
Read Colossians 1:22-23

- **?** *What three things does Jesus give to those who are reconciled to him (v 22)?*
- **?** *How does this reconciliation happen in practical terms (v 23)?*
- **?** *What is required of us (v 23)?*

It might seem that these "conditions" placed the responsibility back on us. But Paul's argument here is not about our *efforts* but about our *dependence*. Our faith is both established and firm. But it is ground that we must not shift from. Jesus is the one who has done it all, so it is madness to move away from him and to put our trust in other things—a theme we will return to in Colossians 2.

Pray

Thank God that you have been rescued from your past and have a glorious future that is secure. Pray that you would continue to trust him in the here and now.

The secret disclosed

We all love a mystery. Something inexplicable happens, and our minds are drawn to try and work out what happened, whodunit, what the solution is.

For thousands of years the gospel was a mystery. There were hints and rumours. There were suggestions and shadows. God forgave his people, and yet how could the blood of an animal atone for the sins of a human? It was a mystery. What were God's plans for the world outside of Israel? Were these non-Jewish people just all to be discarded? It was a mystery.

Revealed

Read Colossians 1:24-27

❓ *What was the commission given to Paul (v 25)?*
❓ *Who has God chosen to reveal the "mystery" to?*
❓ *What is the mystery (v 27)?*
❓ *Why is this mystery so shocking to the Jews?*

What Paul offers at the end of this paragraph is a summary of this treasure more succinct than any tweet and more momentous than any sound bite. For he summarises the privilege of being a Christian in its entirety in just seven words: "Christ in you—the hope of glory". The "you" here refers specifically Gentile Christians.

God no longer lives in the Jerusalem Temple—which excluded Gentiles, the vast majority of people who live in the world—but he has taken up residence in anyone who hears the gospel message and responds.

Christ living within us is the foundation of our confidence. He makes the difference between worldly hope and Christian hope. Worldly hope is wishful thinking—of the sort that hopes for an Aston Martin or an all-expenses-paid tropical holiday at Christmas. It might happen, but it is very unlikely.

Christian hope is light years from that—it is full of confidence. Why? Because it does not depend on "me" in the slightest. It is only because of Christ. How else could I expect to enter God's glorious presence? I need the glorious riches of his revealed gospel. Only Christ can get me there. So I can truly say that he will get me there—because he promises to take us all the way.

☑ Apply

❓ *"Christ in you, the hope of glory." What excites you about this summary of the gospel message and the benefit from it?*
❓ *What enabled Paul to persevere and even rejoice in his suffering (v 24)? Why do we find it difficult to feel the same way?*

Turn your answers into both prayer and praise.

Galaxies and giraffes

In Psalm 146 it is an individual who is praising God. Psalm 147 has the assembled people of God praising their Lord. Now the focus shifts again...

Read Psalm 148

Celestial praise

Read Psalm 148:1-6 again

❷ Who does the psalmist say should praise God (2-4)?

❷ Why should they do this (v 5-6)?

The discoveries that scientists are making about the universe are simply amazing. The photographs of the beauty and splendour of the galaxies from the Hubble Space Telescope make you draw your breath. And yet, the description of how God did it all in Genesis 1:16b is delightfully low-key: "He also made the stars".

···· **TIME OUT** ································

❷ How should we respond to people who take an unhealthy interest in their "stars". What would the Psalmist say to them?

Terrestrial praise

Read Psalm 148:7-12 again

❷ Who exactly is called upon now to praise God?

❷ Who is not included in this list?

Exactly no-one and nothing is excluded! The *whole of the planet earth* owes a debt and a duty of praise and honour to its Creator.

Rational praise

Read Psalm 148:13-14 again

❷ What is astonishing about what verse 14 says after saying the words of verse 13?

We are to praise God (v 13) because he has shown us what he is like. We know his name—which tells us about his character.

We are also to praise God (v 14a) because he has raised up a people (saints) and a king for them. That is the significance of the "horn": a strong leader—a king who is also a deliverer, a saviour.

And we are to praise God (v 14b) because he loves us. God is not so consumed with his own glory and greatness that he excludes others from it. Quite the contrary. his purpose for his people is for them to share in his glory for ever. All the more reason to adore him.

⌄ Apply

Have you been having a tough time recently? Are you tired? Fed up? Struggling? Worried? Psalm 148 tells us that we should praise him whatever our circumstances. You may find it difficult, but do it now...

❷ How do verses 13 and 14 encourage you to do that?

How to be a servant

Wanted: Men and women of any age, background or experience to share the greatest news in the world. Hard work. Imprisonment and suffering probable. Death certain.

It's not a great job advert. And yet that was the reality of becoming a Christian in Paul's day. And it's also the same reality in many parts of the world in our day as well.

The gospel

Read Colossians 1:28

❷ *What is the content of the gospel message, according to verse 28?*

❷ *How should we present it to others and to each other?*

❷ *What do you think "admonishing" and "teaching ... with all wisdom" mean?*

Admonishing literally means "straightening out". Of course, such correction should never be done in a spirit of pride because none of us can ever grasp Christ fully. We all need others to help us keep on the straight and narrow—both in our thinking and understanding and in how we live.

Teaching about God is a tall order! This is why Paul maintains that he does this with "all wisdom". He is not referring to human wisdom or worldly wisdom. This wisdom can only be a work of God.

As Paul prayed for the Colossians back in 1:9, there is a continuous need for filling "with the knowledge of his will through all the wisdom and understanding that the Spirit gives". But the impact on the hearers ultimately rests with God—it is his Spirit that brings wisdom and understanding, as eyes are opened and hearts softened.

⌄ Apply

❷ *Do you talk about Jesus? Or about something else—philosophy, church, "God" in a vague kind of way? How can help yourself to focus on Jesus more?*

❷ *Think about how you could humbly and carefully rebuke another believer about their thinking or behaviour. Why do we find this difficult to do?*

❷ *Pray that those who teach and lead in your church would do so with godly wisdom and insight.*

The cost

Read Colossians 1:28-29

❷ *What is the ultimate aim we should have in sharing the gospel message with others?*

❷ *How hard is this work?*

❷ *Where does the strength come from?*

We slog... and he sustains. But it helps when we are clear about the basics. Jesus is our message. Our aim is to bring people to maturity in Christ for eternity.

⌃ Pray

Pray that this would be your aim and the aim of those in your church who lead. Pray they would work hard and rely on God.

Protective measures

In Colossians 2 Paul will go on to talk about the threats to a Christian's maturity in Christ. But as with any disease, the best cure is prevention...

Read Colossians 2:1-5

> ❓ *What does Paul want for the Christians he knows and does not know?*
> ❓ *Why is his prayer for these things so urgent (v 4)?*

Objectives like encouragement and unity trip off the tongue so easily that they can quickly become clichés. So Paul has to contend in prayer for them. That is not simply because it is hard to keep praying and working for people you have never met, but also because neither encouragement nor unity come easily. They have to be fought for. C.S. Lewis once said, "Everyone thinks forgiveness is a lovely idea until he has something to forgive". Something similar could be said for unity—it's a lovely idea until we find something to divide over. That is when loving a brother or sister in Christ becomes a challenge. Furthermore,

the implication is that unity is related to how "encouraged in heart" we might be. This is not the limp idea of generally feeling upbeat; the phrase has the sense of being strengthened and fortified—literally, being instilled with courage.

Apply

> ❓ *How do encouragement, unity and understanding prevent us from being deceived?*
> ❓ *How would you put Paul's prayer priorities in the diagram below into your own words?*

Pray

Use Paul's pattern below to pray for two people you know, and two Christians you have never met before.

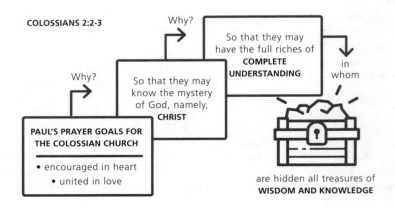

The secret of growth

What is the secret of growing into maturity as a Christian? Paul will go on to talk about three false ways, but first he presents the real way…

As you received…

Read Colossians 2:6

❓ *How does Paul describe how to become a Christian here?*

"I received Christ Jesus as Lord". The words might trip off the tongue, but they contain a wealth of detail. "Christ Jesus" tells us that we are committed to someone who actually lived in history—not an idea, a story or a myth but a living, breathing person. And the belief that he is "Lord" is our conviction that he is God's chosen King and Lord of all. But more than that, becoming a Christian is *personal*. We "receive" him. It is not just ticking off a list of facts we believe about Christ. It is receiving him personally into our lives that makes us true Christians.

… continue

Read Colossians 2:6 again

❓ *What is the secret of going on in the Christian life?*

Paul's word in verse 6 often translated "live" literally means "walk". We are to continue walking with him and in him. The secret of *growing* as a Christian is precisely the same as *becoming* a Christian: daily receiving Christ Jesus as Lord and living out the implications of that. John Stott used to say that we should each "daily bewail our sin and daily adore our Saviour".

Rooted and built up

Read Colossians 2:6-7

❓ *What two pictures of growing as a Christian does Paul use in verse 7?*
❓ *What does he say the experience of living as a believer should be?*

Grounded. Convinced. Unshakable. Thankful. These are the marks of a mature Christian believer. With strong roots, like a mature tree, we will not be blown over by a hurricane. Like a well-built house, we will have strong foundations and remain standing even when an earthquake rocks us.

Paul uses one further metaphor from the natural world—a river that has burst its banks. The torrents of rainwater are unstoppable and they flow wherever they can. Likewise, the gratitude of those who have received Christ Jesus as Lord knows no bounds. But perhaps that seems unrealistic—especially when life is hard or confusing. How could gratitude overflow then? The answer is because of what motivates that gratitude: the privilege and wonder of knowing Christ and his grace.

⌄ Apply

❓ *On these criteria and by these measures are you growing as a Christian?*

Spend some time expressing your overflowing gratitude to God.

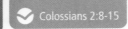
Fake news

Paul now turns to some of the storms that seek to undermine our confident faith in Christ. He introduces them with a summary statement of what is at stake.

Hollow and deceptive

Read Colossians 2:8

- ❓ *How does Paul describe the things that threaten to knock us off course as Christians?*
- ❓ *What is the fundamental flaw with them?*
- ❓ *Why might these things be so deceptive— even for Christians?*

Fly fishing rests on pure deception. A replica of an insect is flicked over the surface of the river, luring an unsuspecting fish into rising to the surface for the next tasty insect morsel. The more convincing the fly, the better it will work. So it is with the fake news of false teaching. If it didn't resemble the real thing, people would never be taken in. What resembles good food is actually a trap. It promises the earth but delivers nothing. It is all surface with little substance.

It may come with the weight of substantial human traditions behind it: magnificent buildings and an impressive history. It may come with a sense of real "spiritual power" about it. But at the end of the day it does not rest on Christ.

The real deal

Read Colossians 2:9-15

- ❓ *What arguments does Paul use to show how superior Jesus is to the fake alternatives?*

- ❓ *What has happened to us as believers joined to Christ (v 12)?*
- ❓ *What three enemies are destroyed by Jesus' death on the cross (v 13-15)? How has this been achieved?*

Paul piles on the arguments, starting with a recap of his statements about who Jesus is from Colossians 1. The mention of circumcision here perhaps reflects that the Christians were being pulled away by false Jewish teaching. He explains that the only circumcision that matters is the one that we receive in Christ—we are spiritually joined in Christ to the people of God. We are made alive in Christ as we join him in his death and his resurrection. We were forgiven *all* our sins (2:13). And the impressive spiritual powers that lie behind alternative philosophies were defeated utterly by Christ on the cross. The implication is clear. Tempting though they are, why would you want to swap Jesus for them?

⌄ Apply

- ❓ *What human philosophies and traditions do you think you and your church are particularly vulnerable to believing? How do they tempt us into thinking that Jesus is not enough?*
- ❓ *What kinds of things are we tempted to "add" to faith in Christ in order to give us more assurance? What is the antidote to these claims?*

Legalists and mystics

False teaching attacks our heads, hearts or hands. Wrong thinking. Wrong feelings. Or a wrong attitude towards the significance of what we do with our bodies.

Don't judge me!
Read Colossians 2:16-17

❓ *What do the things listed in verse 16 have in common?*

❓ *What do you imagine the situation is in Colossae, from verse 16?*

❓ *Why would the Christians find that difficult?*

❓ *What should they say to themselves and their accusers (v 17)?*

These practices were all issues touched on in the old covenant. In their different ways, each of these were the means for Old Testament believers to show their devotion to, and dependence on, their rescuer God. It proved they were different from their pagan neighbours, for whom such laws were irrelevant. It couldn't help but set them apart. So in a sense, the whole point was that people *did* judge believers by these things! If you didn't follow these rules, people would naturally assume you were not part of the devout in-crowd. But now Paul suggests that none of it matters anymore. They were just the shadows, and the reality is Christ. When you have the real thing, you don't need the shadow.

▼ Apply

❓ *Perhaps we are not troubled by Jewish laws and rituals, but what are some of the rules we lay on each other?*

❓ *What should we say to ourselves and our accusers when we are judged?*

Don't disqualify me!
Read Colossians 2:18-19

❓ *What are the twin practises that Paul talks about here?*

❓ *Why might believers feel threatened by these things?*

❓ *What is Paul's conclusion about those who encourage these things?*

Verse 18 refers not to worshipping angels—no true Christian would be tempted by that—but the claim to worship *alongside* angels. In other words, these people were experiencing a profound intimacy with God through their times of worship, and so they argued that those who didn't join in with them were truly missing out. The suggestion is that they went through elaborate, self-denying processes (extended periods of fasting or extra-long prayer times perhaps) in order to enter into the "right space" for worship and participate in a higher kind of worship. This is a kind of mystical experience available only to those dedicated to going through all the right techniques. But in doing so, Paul says, they have lost connection with Christ. We are already in him and he is in us. No rituals, no special experiences, no self denial is needed. We live and move in his presence all the time.

▲ Pray

Enjoy the full and free access to God the Father that you have in Christ now.

Dead but alive

Legalism is alive and well—if not in our churches, then in a corner of our minds. It is the voice that tells us, "If you don't do this or that, you're not a real believer…"

Dead to law

Read Colossians 2:20-23

- ❷ *What does Paul say has happened to all Christians?*
- ❷ *What are the implications of this for how we think about rules?*
- ❷ *What particular rules does Paul seem to have in mind (v 21-22)?*
- ❷ *What two big reasons or principles does Paul give in verse 22 to reject these rules?*
- ❷ *What is so attractive about these rules (v 23)?*

Of course, it's rarely that simple. Many of the rules, practices and customs that build up around our expectations of what Christian spirituality and discipleship look like have their origins in scripture. And skilled exponents will make a wise case for why we must fall in line. But even if such rules have their origins in Scripture, legalism twists them into something thoroughly worldly. They are "based on merely human commands and teachings". They will perish because they are past their sell-by date. They are from a past era: the shadow times. But now the mystery has been revealed and we live with the reality—Christ.

☑ Apply

So here's the shock: it *is worldly to be religious!* This is why religious legalism should be entirely out of place for the Christian believer. We are to enjoy our security and freedom and not regress back to the old way of thinking.

But this is hard, precisely because the legalistic mindset runs so deeply within us. Countering it sometimes needs conscious efforts—the deliberate decision to resist the accusing voices of our minds that try to convince us of divine disappointment and thus our spiritual jeopardy. We must stop ourselves. We must say to ourselves, *No! That's just worldliness! God's love for me does not depend on my spiritual and moral performance! It depends on Christ dying for me.*

This is a lifelong battle—so we should not be caught by surprise. Legalism is normal and ingrained thinking. But it is emphatically not Christian thinking.

The irony of legalism

Read Colossians 2:23

- ❷ *Why does legalism ultimately fail?*

If we imagine that we can control our most sinful impulses and desires by being obsessively religious, and can do so without Christ, then Paul has strong words for us. *It won't work.* Observers might greatly respect us (as the people of Jesus' time did the Pharisees). Or they might despise us and assume that we are perfectly insane. Either way, this approach is proved to be utterly pointless.

The singing swordsman

This psalm divides neatly into two halves: the first is easier; the second is a bit more tricky!

Read Psalm 149

People with a song

❓ *From verses 1-5 list what God wants his people to do.*
❓ *What is so exciting about God and what he has given (v 2, 4)?*

Notice that the praise of God should be something that is fresh. That's the significance of the new song (v 1) that we are encouraged to sing. Being creative about how we praise God is an appropriate response to our creating, redeeming God. Notice that it's not just reserved for the assembly either (v 5).

⬇ Apply

Why not make praising the Living Lord the last thing you do tonight as you settle down in bed (v 5b).

Stuck in a rut? It sometimes helps to use the words of hymns or poems to refresh our praise. Check out some good new hymn books (or rediscover some old ones), and use the words to encourage and express your praises to God.

People with a sword
Read Psalm 149:6-9 again

❓ *How might the first readers/singers of this psalm have understood these verses?*

❓ *How would Christians today understand them differently? (Hint: see how the phrase "double-edged sword" from v 6 is used in the New Testament in Hebrews 4:12-13.)*

A curious mixture—a song and a sword. This psalm was written to God's Old Testament people: the nation of Israel. And Israel was often called on by God to take action against those who had rejected his rule.

So sword talk wasn't odd here: God's people were celebrating that God is just. Those who rejected him would not go unpunished (Psalm 149:9), and God would use his people as agents of that judgment.

But now, God's people are no longer a physical nation; we are found in *every* nation. And the "double-edged sword" is the word of God, which God's people are still called to wield. So, when the Bible's message is announced to those who are not Christians, we not only announce God's rescue but also his judgment too. Serious stuff.

⬇ Apply

❓ *What's the message that you're passing on to your non-Christian friends and neighbours?*
❓ *Does it include both God's love and justice?*

Praise God for verse 4, and for the job he has given us to do.

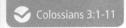
A new address

"Where are you from?" It is the first question we ask on meeting someone who seems "different". Christians have a radical answer to that question.

Where are you?

Read Colossians 3:1-4

❓ *Where do Christians live now?*
❓ *How did we get there?*
❓ *When will what we are be finally revealed?*
❓ *How does Paul say this truth should shape our thinking?*

When Jesus rose from the dead, those in Christ rose with him. Where he goes, we go. The extraordinary thing is that because Jesus then ascended to his heavenly throne and sat down, we have too. In Christ, we are in heaven. Already. That is our true home. It is only natural, therefore, to seek after what Paul literally calls "the above things" (v 2). This must include the things that make the heavenly realms so wonderful, joyful and magnetic: the wonder of spending time with Christ, the one we love and adore—everything that flows from being in the place "where Christ is". So Paul instructs the Colossians to set their hearts on these things. This means to meditate on them, value them, prioritise them. Above all, let them shape and influence life in the here and now.

Apply

❓ *Write down all the "identities" you possess (nationality, job, relationships, etc.). Honestly, put them in the order*

they seem most important to you. Where does your identity in Christ sit in the list? Why is that, and how can it be made the highest priority?

A new wardrobe

Read Colossians 3:5-11

❓ *Why is it important to understand the lessons on legalism in Colossians 2 as we read these verses?*
❓ *What three pictures does Paul use to show us how to live as new people in Christ (3:5, 7, 8-9)?*
❓ *What do the things listed in verses 5 and 8-9 have in common?*

Growing as a Christian is not so much about desperately trying to stop doing things. It is primarily about seeing what Christ has done for and in us, and realising that we are dead to the old things. We now walk in a different direction. We have taken off our old clothes and put on some glorious new ones to wear to the Lamb's wedding feast. Paul is saying: *Be who you are.* Nowhere is this new way of living clearer than in our attitudes towards sex and in how we speak: in our relationships with others.

Pray

Thank God for who he has made you in Christ; and talk to him about the lists in verses 5 and 8-9.

A new family

We do not seek to grow in holiness out of fear. Fear is what religion provokes, because it stirs up anxiety about what God might do to us when we fail.

Christians long to grow in holiness *out of confidence*—we belong to God because we are united to Christ. It is simply a matter of being who we have been saved to be.

Relationships

Read Colossians 3:8-11

❓ *What does verse 11 add to the perspective that Paul is building up of our new life in Christ?*

❓ *How do you think Paul's original hearers might have responded to verse 11?*

The proof of the Christian's conversion is in their interactions with others. It is almost impossible to grow as a disciple in isolation. But the church fellowship is not simply formed of other people who are like us. The church was never designed to be a club for like-minded or same-cultured people. Jesus is frustratingly unfussy about who he chooses and loves. He does not discriminate, which is why it is worse than a tragedy when Christians do. It suggests we think we are somehow superior to some of those for whom Christ died—as if we were more deserving somehow, when the truth is that none of us deserve for it to be this good.

We easily lose sight of how revolutionary verse 11 really is. Our connection to Christ puts all other identities in their place—no matter how proud or patriotic we may be, our first kingdom is always the kingdom of Christ: King Jesus is all.

Realities

Read Colossians 3:12-14

❓ *How does it help our relationships with others to know that we are chosen... holy... dearly loved (v 12)?*

❓ *What practical reality regarding relationships is Paul pointing to in these verses?*

There are always going to be members of the church community who require from us very big hearts if we are to put up with them. People can be irritating, frustrating, hurtful and cutting—*and so can you!* And you will be painfully aware that forgiveness is easier to think about than it is to actually do. That's why Paul points us to our own need for forgiveness and the example of our Lord Jesus, who sacrificed all for our forgiveness (v 13). We so desperately need the love of God poured into our hearts for each other.

⌄ Apply

❓ *Endure, forgive, love... Which of these do people find hardest to do in your fellowship? Why is it so corrosive to a church's life and witness when these things are not practised?*

⌃ Pray

Ask God to help you love others, and that your church would model the things we have read about today.

How to do church

In a Christian community, we are not shaped by rules, but we are shaped by our Ruler. But his rule is unlike any other. It is a rule of genuine peace.

True peace

Read Colossians 3:15-17

❓ *What do you think it means to "let the peace of Christ rule in [our] hearts"?*
❓ *How does that happen among us, according to verse 16?*
❓ *What is the repeated command in these verses? Why do you think that is?*

Conflict will always arise when two or more people are together. But conflict among believers is not by itself the problem, but the way it gets handled can be. The key in Paul's mind here seems to be Christ's peace ruling "in your hearts". This is not super-spiritual escapism, as if we simply need to meditate on Jesus and feel peaceful before an argument. Since the heart is the source of all those passions and lusts which cause so many problems in the world, and which Paul referred to in verses 5-9, he is saying that Christ must rule there. The peace he achieved on the cross to reconcile us to God and to each other must be the decisive factor in any dispute.

The mindset of gratitude has been one of the letter's consistent themes (look back to 1:12 and 2:7). It is wholly appropriate here. If every individual involved in a church dispute insisted on returning to what he or she was thankful to God for, it would guarantee that their relationships would be profoundly improved. It would put our identity in Christ centre stage—and thereby make it more likely that people would bear with and forgive one another (3:13). And essential to the whole process is that we are sitting under the gospel message together—"the message of Christ".

True worship

Read Colossians 3:15-17 again

❓ *What is practically involved in letting the message of Christ dwell in us richly?*
❓ *What role does Paul say singing should play in our life together?*

There should be a horizontal as well as a vertical dimension to our singing. We sing to God of course, with gratitude in our hearts. But there should also be a way that the words of the songs shape our thinking, and even rebuke us for our sinful behaviour. Notice also that *variety* in singing was important right from the beginning.

⌄ Apply

❓ *What are the three ingredients for a healthy Christian life (v 15, 16, 17)? How do you think you match up to these criteria? What about your church?*

⌃ Pray

Ask God to help you enjoy and be an agent of his peace as you meet with your brothers and sisters this week.

How to do family

*To our ears, these brief but punchy commands may seem dated and even dangerous. This is why we need to see what Paul is and, more significantly, is **not** saying.*

Home truths

Household codes were not unusual in the ancient world. But they shared one thing in common: women, slaves and children were all "owned"—the father was the undisputed authority in the home.

Read Colossians 3:18 – 4:1

❓ *What is the common thread that runs through these commands (3:18, 20, 22-23)?*

❓ *What are the big surprises in verses 19, 21 and 22?*

In cities around the Roman world, women (v 18) and slaves (v 22-24), and their children (v 20), were being converted. God was at work among them. Not only that: God was using women and slaves, and no doubt also children, to further his kingdom. So just as Jesus did before him, Paul shows them the respect due to those with minds and wills of their own. This was revolutionary. No one had ever done that before. Every previous household code had been addressed deliberately and exclusively to the male head of the house. Furthermore, Paul addresses each of these less powerful groups first.

A word to Dad

Read Colossians 3:18 – 4:1 again

❓ *What role does the father have in the household?*

❓ *Who is true head of the household?*

A pagan teacher would give all kinds of helpful tips for how such a man could get the best out of the household team. That might include treating his subordinates well enough so that they would do what he wanted. But the emphasis was consistent: it helped *him* keep order among *them*. There's not a bit of this with Paul. *Not once*—either here or in his other household codes—does Paul ever tell the men to *make* the women, children or slaves do *anything*. This is a fact overlooked by too many men who rule their homes like petty dictators, even justifying physical violence on the basis of these verses. They want to force everyone else to bend to their will. Instead, Paul gives some profoundly challenging and even subversive instructions to the men. They are not the head of the household: Jesus is. And we all play out our roles in submission to Christ.

⌄ Apply

❓ *Identify one personal relationship you are struggling with at the moment. What command from these verses do you most need to hear and work through right now?*

❓ *How does the centrality of Jesus to all our relationships change everything?*

Prayer and partnership

We have access to God in prayer by the grace we have received in Christ. Why then do we so often find it difficult to pray?

Devoted

Read Colossians 4:2

> ❓ *What do you think it means in practice to "devote yourself to prayer"?*
> ❓ *What do you think being watchful involves?*

Yet again, Paul is not laying down the law here. He is not offering a list of rules and regulations by which we can measure our efforts; for prayerfulness can only be motivated by a response to God's grace. That's why we want to spend time with God! That's why Paul uses a word like "devote" (v 2). It suggests our sincere passion as much as our deliberate purpose. Sometimes there is a battle between our passion and our purpose, when we are distracted by other things that might be good in themselves to do but that drag us away from our prayer times. What matters is that we each find a way to spend time in prayer, using whatever methods that genuinely help. There are no rules, but we can develop good disciplines.

⌄ Apply

Prayer doesn't need to be in a closed room. You can pray when out for a walk, using a list or a smartphone app to keep a record of your prayer commitments.

> ❓ *What's the best place for you to pray? If you struggle to make the time, work out why that is and come up with a solution.*

Praying for the gospel

Read Colossians 4:3-6

> ❓ *For what does Paul ask prayers for in his mission to proclaim the gospel?*
> ❓ *What other advice does Paul give us for how we relate to "not-yet Christians"?*
> ❓ *What is the implication of Paul's use of the word "conversation" in verse 6?*

Paul wants opportunities (open doors) to share the good news about Jesus. But he also wants clarity when he is speaking. How much we need the same things ourselves! But he also knows that it is God who gives these things, and that it is God's work to make new disciples of Christ. Paul expects people to talk with family, friends and neighbours. He longs for us to feel as comfortable with talking about Jesus as we might about our jobs or the sports results. Conversation implies dialogue and mutual interest, which hopefully means saying things that prompt questions. "Seasoned with salt" seems to have been an old Jewish idiom for keeping things interesting. That can be through being quirky, or provocative, or surprising. The key is to avoid being predictable or banal, because we long for conversation to lead to a new recognition that Christ is indeed Lord.

⌃ Pray

Pray for open doors, clarity and fruitful conversations.

The gospel team

The theme of this letter have been cosmic: Jesus Christ, the image of God, who is Lord of all. But the application is always personal and relational...

Unity and diversity

Read Colossians 4:7-18

❓ *Despite Paul and Aristarchus being in prison, what is the tone and feel of this last section of the letter? What do you put that down to?*

❓ *What is striking about the people Paul mentions? Think about their names and backgrounds.*

❓ *What is sad about verse 14 (see 2 Timothy 4:10)?*

There is not a hint of self pity here. Paul does not ask that they pray for him to be let out. He is simply bubbling over with enthusiasm and delight in the group of Christians God has pulled around him, which means the gospel mission goes on. Tychichus may have had a lot of other things to tell them (Colossians 4:7), but none of these details is as important as the contents of the letter.

The gospel team in Ephesus (the likely place Paul was in prison), and in the churches of Colossae and Laodicea contains a wonderful mix of people that puts the truth of 3:11 on display. Three Jewish men (v 10-11); three Gentiles (Epaphras, Luke and Demas)— probably Greek. Onesimus the runaway slave, and then the women at Colossae, including Nympha (v 15). All are spoken to and of on a level playing field. We are all one in Christ Jesus.

The sad fact is that Demas, at some stage,

fell away. Even those at the very heart of a thriving gospel ministry are vulnerable to temptation.

⌄ Apply

❓ *How diverse is your church? What might be the reasons for this?*

❓ *How does Epaphras' prayer in verse 12 sum up what the letter is about?*

A summary prayer

Read Colossians 4:12

Epaphras' prayer is one that we might use for everyone we know: that Christians would stand firm, grow into maturity, and have complete assurance of the truth of the gospel and their unity with Christ. God's grace can only provoke our gratitude to God. And our gratitude must surely work out in graciousness to one and all, whether to those who are part of the body, or towards outsiders who ply us with questions.

Grace. Gratitude. Graciousness. This is lordship the like of which the world has never seen. What an extraordinary privilege to know it first hand. So as Christ has shared his grace with us, we, with Paul, share grace with all.

⌃ Pray

Use Epaphras' prayer as a model to pray for those you know.

A festival of praise

The last of the Hallelujah Psalms is also the end of the book of Psalms, and it gives a fitting summary of where, why and how we should praise the Lord.

Read Psalm 150

Where?

The sanctuary here is God's temple, which symbolised God's presence among his people.

❷ *How would you apply what verse 1 says today?*

If you said that God should be praised in a church building (sanctuary) and in the world (for example, by singing in the open air)... then sorry, but you get no points. Because the New Testament equivalent of the temple of God is not a church building, but the people of God.

God now dwells in his people—who are themselves the temple of God (see 1 Corinthians 3:16-17). So the correct implication for us is that God's praise should be real, internal and meaningful—irrespective of how we express it outwardly (see Ephesians 5:19).

And praising God in the world isn't about singing hymns in the high street—it's about making his person, character and works known to those who have not heard about him.

Why?

❷ *List four reasons from Psalm 150:1-2 why we give praise to God.*

1. _____

2. _____

3. _____

4. _____

❷ *Can you give some concrete examples for the two reasons in verse 2?*

How?

Actually, this is the least important question, although the list given in verses 3-5 here should liberate us in how we view what "praising the Lord" can encompass.

❷ *What and who are called on to praise God in these verses?*

❷ *Have you been guilty of too narrow a view of how we can and should praise our great God?*

⌄ Apply

Go on then! Time for your own personal "Hallelujah moment"! But make sure it's not just a moment. Make sure the hallelujahs flow into your thinking, your living and your choices this week.

 Bible in a year: Proverbs 19-21 • Hebrews 1

Introduce a friend to

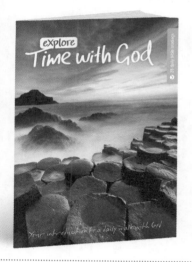

explore

If you're enjoying using *Explore*, why not introduce a friend? *Time with God* is our introduction to daily Bible reading and is a great way to get started with a regular time with God. It includes 28 daily readings along with articles, advice and practical tips on how to apply what the passage teaches.

Why not order a copy for someone you would like to encourage?

Coming up next...

- 1 Timothy
  with Phillip Jensen

- Acts
  with Albert Mohler

- Easter
  with Carl Laferton and Rachel Jones

- Revelation
  with Tim Chester

- Psalms
  with Tim Thornborough

Don't miss your copy. Contact your local Christian bookshop or church agent, or visit:

UK & Europe: thegoodbook.co.uk
info@thegoodbook.co.uk
Tel: 0333 123 0880

North America: thegoodbook.com
info@thegoodbook.com
Tel: 866 244 2165

Australia: thegoodbook.com.au
info@thegoodbook.com.au
Tel: (02) 9564 3555

India: thegoodbook.co.in
info@thegoodbook.co.in
Tel: (+44) 0333 123 0880

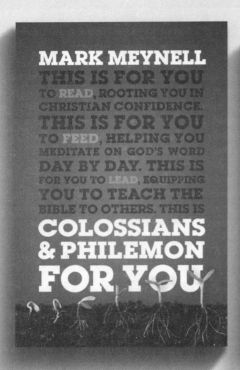

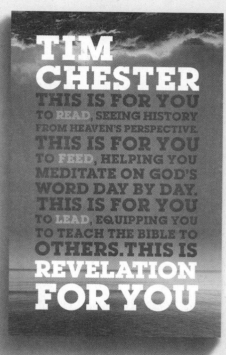

Join the *explore* community

The *Explore* Facebook group is a community of people who use *Explore* to study the Bible each day.

This is the place to share your thoughts, questions, encouragements and prayers as you read *Explore*, and interact with other readers, as well as contributors, from around the world. No questions are too simple or too difficult to ask.

JOIN NOW:
www.facebook.com/groups/tgbc.explore